Revolutionary Learning

Revolutionary Learning

Marxism, Feminism and Knowledge

Sara Carpenter and Shahrzad Mojab

PlutoPress
www.plutobooks.com

First published 2017 by Pluto Press
345 Archway Road, London N6 5AA

www.plutobooks.com

British Library Cataloguing in Publication Data
A catalogue record for this book is available from the British Library

ISBN   978 0 7453 3643 5   Hardback
ISBN   978 0 7453 3638 1   Paperback
ISBN   978 1 7868 0050 3   PDF eBook
ISBN   978 1 7868 0052 7   Kindle eBook
ISBN   978 1 7868 0051 0   EPUB eBook

This book is printed on paper suitable for recycling and made from fully
managed and sustained forest sources. Logging, pulping and manufacturing
processes are expected to conform to the environmental standards of the
country of origin.

Typeset by Stanford DTP Services, Northampton, England

Simultaneously printed in the United Kingdom and United States of America

Contents

Dedication

In memory of Paula Allman, a dear colleague and friend who taught us how to read and use Marx. In preparation for a reading circle and dialogue, Paula sent the following to our group in Toronto in January 2008:

> *To whatever degree you wish, or will permit, I would like to join in the dialogue of your reading circle. Shahrzad has kindly asked me to participate, as far as I can at a distance, but I do not want to impose. Therefore, I hope you will feel free to use, or not use, the following input as you see fit. I also hope that if you want to make any comments to me or ask any questions that you will. I sincerely hope that you all are, or are on your way to becoming, revolutionary critical educators, and both now and in the future I will do everything I can to help you in that endeavour.*

We have the same hopes for our readers as Paula had for us, and we extend the same invitations and wishes.

Acknowledgements

In writing this book we aspired to continue with the ideas posed in our co-edited book, *Educating from Marx: Race, Gender, and Learning* (2011), and in *Marxism and Feminism* (edited by Shahrzad Mojab, 2015). However, this writing required fortitude, as we wanted to go beyond the continuity and think through possibilities for renewal and the resynthesizing of Marxism, feminism, consciousness, ideology, learning and praxis. We tried out our ideas in conversations with our graduate students and colleagues, especially the incomparable Helen Colley, with activists and artists, in Marxist Reading Groups, and in forums in different regions of the world. Thus, this collection is also a reflection of the contributions, critiques and comments of others, whose ideas are entwined with ours and have inspired us. We feel especially indebted to Paula Allman, Himani Bannerji and Dorothy Smith, whose scholarly rigour has helped us in thinking through the complex subject matters of Marx's method, capitalist social relations, imperialism, colonialism, feminism and anti-racism.

We gratefully thank Stephan Dobson for his unwavering interest in our writings and his consistent editorial and theoretical reminder to avoid 'tripping' the readers!

We are grateful to a number of individuals at Pluto Press for their assistance and support. Our deep appreciation goes to David Shulman for his unflagging support and encouragement.

We offer deep and tender thanks to Amir Hassanpour, who has generously provided invaluable personal and scholarly support over the years.

Versions of some of the chapters included here were originally published in other formats and have been revised and expanded:

Chapter 2 appeared as S. Carpenter and S. Mojab, 'What is "critical" about critical adult education?', in T. Nesbit, S. Brigham, N. Taber and T. Gibb (eds.), *Building on critical traditions: Adult education and learning in Canada* (Toronto: Thompson, 2013), pp. 160–70.

Chapter 3 appeared as S. Carpenter and S. Mojab, 'The "matter" of consciousness in Marxist-Feminist theory', in P. Jones (ed.), *Marxism and Education: Dialogues on Pedagogy and Culture* (New York: Palgrave Macmillan, 2011), pp. 117–40.

Chapter 4 appeared as S. Carpenter, 'Centering Marxist-Feminism in adult learning', *Adult Education Quarterly*, Vol. 62, No. 1, 2012, 19–35, available at http://aeq.sagepub.com/content/62/1/19.full.pdf+html.

Chapter 7 is derived in part from an article published in the *International Journal of Lifelong Education*, 26 July 2011, available at http://www.tandfonline.com/doi/full/10.1080/02601370.2011.588466

We thank the editors and publishers for permission to republish earlier versions of the chapters. Portions of this research were supported by the Social Sciences and Humanities Research Council of Canada. We fully understand that we alone are responsible for all the ideas presented in this text.

1

Introduction:
Revolutionary Feminist Praxis

It is now an intellectual and political habit for us to begin our writing with the assertion that the world is messy and chaotic. The more we open our essays with this statement, the messier the world gets. Millions of people are driven to the seas and through the deserts by wars, destruction, dispossession and displacement. Aspirations to live free of violence are difficult to realize in the context of the vast, persistent and growing inequities of Europe and North America, compounded by increasingly reactionary and racist violence on the part of the state and civil society against forcibly displaced people. The persistence of this material condition is utterly dependent on the ideologies of patriarchal, racist capitalist social relations. Under the global expression of racialized patriarchy, violence has increased exponentially, taking on a massified character and regularly reported around the world: the rape to death of women in public, including by military, paramilitary and extremist forces; their abduction and selling in the sex market; the enforcement of child marriage; sexual abuse and assault from refugee camps to university campuses; arrest and imprisonment of Palestinian girls and women for their resistance to occupation; the detainment of Kurdish women activists in Turkey; the missing and murdered indigenous women in Canada; the murder of women on the US–Mexico Border; girls kidnapped across Africa; and religious forms of terrorism against women's reproductive autonomy. These are breath-taking atrocities committed every day and night by patriarchal forces of capitalism, imperialism and fundamentalisms. As Bannerji argues, 'the very content of the word "human" is being emptied out and filled with screams of agony of those condemned to it. In this atmosphere of violence how can violence against women not intensify, almost as an excrescence of this ordered disorder?' (2016, p. 17).

In order to address not only these forms of violence and degradation, but also the continuing contradictions of patriarchal, racist capitalism,

1

we argue that we need to *revolutionize* our thinking around learning and the critical education project. We consider this endeavour to be our contribution as revolutionary feminist scholars of education. By revolutionize, we do not simply mean change: we need to fully embrace the revolutionary potential of learning and pedagogical work and engage with our history of scholarship through the imperative of generating revolutionary feminist praxis. By praxis we mean, following Allman's dialectical articulation, 'a concept that grasps the *internal relation* between *consciousness* and sensuous human experience, a unity of opposites that reciprocally shape and determine one another' (2007, p. 79, emphasis in original). We explore this dialectical iteration of praxis through this text. It is our contention – and we would argue these claims can easily be seen in the last three decades of debate – that critical education is plagued by persistent theoretical and political inconsistencies. Following significant articulations of the relation between education and social reproduction, the field of critical education has been unable to contend with the growing complexity of both the material condition of the world and the ideological apparatus of bourgeois society in the academy. As argued by key Marxist scholars of education, including Paula Allman, Wayne Au, Noah De Lissovoy, Teresa Ebert, Sandy Grande, John Holst and Glenn Rikowski, critical education theory suffers from several important inconsistencies and reformist tendencies. The influence of a non-dialectical reading of Marx under conditions of patriarchy and racism continues to produce substantial errors in scholarship, including: the inability to understand class and labour power as relations and processes; a causal and deterministic articulation of consciousness and praxis as external relations; culturalist and identity-based approaches to 'difference' that cannot illuminate inter-constitutive social relations; confusion over the relationality between colonialism, fundamentalisms, imperialism and neoliberalism within capitalism; and the continued marginalization of feminist, anti-racist and anti-colonial scholarship within the academy. This position has left critical education theory stuck in economistic, reformist and culturalist cycles, unable to contend with the aggressive tendencies of both liberalism and the veiled bourgeois project of post- and identity theories. Or, as Bannerji has argued in a discussion of her own feminist praxis, we see a clear need to overcome 'a binary and inverse relationship between "class" and "culture", or "discourse" and "social relations", structure and forms of consciousness, which seems to pervade our intellectual world' (2001, p. 9).

This book is both a collection of previous work and a reflection on our own struggle to understand 'revolutionary learning'. It includes pieces informed by multiple conversations with different scholars over the last ten years. This reading is deeply influenced by Paula Allman's theorization of consciousness and praxis (1999, 2001, 2007), the epistemological work of Dorothy E. Smith (1988, 1990, 1999, 2011), and Himani Bannerji's Marxist feminist theorization of race, gender and class (1995, 2000, 2001, 2011, 2015, 2016). The text represents an ongoing engagement with the deepening of our theoretical and empirical work around the question of consciousness and praxis in educational theory and is informed by our intellectual and political praxis in feminist, anti-colonial and anti-racist struggles. Over the years, this engagement has resulted in extensive writing, both published and unpublished, and this process has helped us deepen our grasp of the theoretical tools necessary to make sense of the relations of ruling. This includes consciousness and praxis, but also the concepts of learning, education, experience, community, reform, revolution, social relations, dialectics, racism, colonialism, materialism and patriarchy, among others. In each chapter, we endeavour to get closer to the key concepts we need to understand. As such, conceptually there is some overlap between the chapters, but they are a record and reflection of our own struggle to learn and to sharpen our understanding of both the theorization and the political implications of this body of work.

We see this book as both continuing and extending the argument offered by Paula Allman. As such, we use her work extensively, but also try to expand her analysis into domains of racialized, patriarchal capitalism. We also intend to follow her thesis that Marx's theory of consciousness and praxis is the most important theoretical core of critical education and, unfortunately, is often ignored, misused and misunderstood by the majority of critical educational scholars. The intellectual lineage of critical education, from Marx to Vygotsky to Gramsci to Freire, read through an ideology that appropriates revolutionary thought for the purposes of reforming existing educational institutions and social relations, necessarily results in the kinds of misunderstandings Allman thoroughly describes. For example, Au (2007) has discussed the misuse of Freire for the purposes of reforming schooling contexts, an appropriation which Freire identified as an ideological inversion of his work. Such misunderstandings result in a theoretical and practical tension between reform and revolution that educational theory cannot resolve without a political commitment to the kind of imagination embodied in this historical project. However, we also contend that critical education theory cannot commit itself to, nor move forward with, a revolutionary project without profound attention to the social relations of difference – that is, gender, race, ability, sexuality – and the exploration of these as inter-constitutive relations both with and within capitalism and its expansion through colonialism and imperialism (this point is developed further in Chapters 6 and 7). Let us be unequivocal on this point: Marxist scholarship on education that ignores important debates in feminism and anti-racist scholarship is itself sexist, racist and, at this historical moment, deeply inadequate to address the condition of life on this planet.

In this chapter, we will expand on these claims by expounding upon the need to revisit the conceptual grounds of critical and radical educational theory. Given the persistent problems in critical education that we have already named, as well as our own intellectual and political commitments, we see an imperative for deeper conceptual work to address the ongoing de-politicization and de-radicalization of critical educational theory. Again, we encourage our readers to engage with these texts as a whole and as a model of our own learning through and as struggle, a revolutionary struggle, towards understanding what constitutes revolutionary learning. This exploration has two major components. We begin this complex elaboration in the section below entitled 'Living in abstractions and thinking through ideology' by expanding on the method of abstraction in our social and material life and forms of consciousness. This argument both grounds and conditions our discussion of the use of the concept of ideology in critical educational theory as an example of some of the conceptual problems internal to the field. In the final section of this chapter, 'Coming back to revolutionary feminism', we draw upon the previous section to articulate our thinking around the relationship between critical educational theory and revolutionary feminist praxis. We conclude this chapter with both a map of the text as a whole and by revisiting the political imperatives that drive this intellectual endeavour.

Living in abstractions and thinking through ideology

All science would be superfluous if the outward appearance and the essence of things directly coincided. (Marx, 1986, p. 817)

In our classrooms, we often introduce our students to the idea that we need to 'think about how we think'. This is a difficult notion for them, often experienced as overly ponderous or just another attempt at forcing 'reflection' or a divulging of their darkest secrets. However, we try, very quickly, to move past this by talking with them about what they ate for breakfast. We do this because we are not just trying to get them to be reflective, but also to think about the relationship between how they experience, on a daily/nightly basis, the material social reality in which they live and how they understand and make sense of that reality. This involves them becoming aware of the fact that they are interpreting the world, that they use theories to interpret the world, that they have a consciousness that is active and also inherited from the past. It also involves, however, helping them to know that there is dissonance, a tension, between our experiential realities and our consciousness, and that that tension is intricately, sometimes paradoxically, bound up in how we think. The problem they must deal with is how to abstract, and it is the same problem that confronts scholars and practitioners of critical and radical forms of education.

We begin with breakfast because it is immediate; it may even still be in their stomachs or just waning away, causing them to be hungry and distracted. It is visceral, present and real. Some of them didn't eat it, and they suffer hunger pains, distraction and fatigue. We ask them to think about the process of obtaining a simple breakfast. In their home, perhaps they make themselves a bowl of cereal. We ask, 'Where did this cereal come from?' The answer: 'The store'. We then ask them to think more closely about this simple act. Where did it come from before the store? What persons have been involved in the production of the box of corn flakes that now (weakly) nourishes their body? Where was the grain grown? Who tended and reaped it? How was it processed? Boxed? Shipped? Unpacked? Presented? In a slightly unnerving turn we ask them, how many people touched your food before you ate it?

At one level of Marxian analysis, as some of our readers might be thinking right now, we can simply call this commodity fetishism. And yes, this is a classic example of this concept. But what, we ask our students, is contained in the concept of 'fetishism?' Fetishism, according to Marx's elaboration, is a specific kind of reification. Reification is a way of thinking that turns processes and relations into *things*. Fetishism is a form of reification in which 'the attributes and powers, the essence, of the person or social relation appear as natural, intrinsic, attributes or powers of the "thing" ... social relations between people are misconstrued as relations between things' (Allman, 2007, p. 37). When we think about our breakfast as something bought and paid for whose entire existence is limited to the store where we purchased it, we express this fetishism. We do not see the social relations embodied in the cereal; we have abstracted the 'thing', cereal, from the relations in which it was produced. Those relations – in the fields or in the processing plants or in the marketing firm – are deemed not necessary to the commodity exchange that is the act of buying cereal; only the costs related to those processes are present in our purchase and collapsed in the notion of exchange and the 'price' we pay. All that is necessarily present has been filtered out.

The lesson, however, cannot end here because something more complicated emerges. What is this filtering out and how does it happen? What causes us to experience something so fundamental to life – our food – in this way? And how are we to understand the contradiction between the experiential reality, the act of buying cereal, and everything that comes before? How can we reconcile and know something about these more complex relations when we do not, ourselves, experience them? What does this distance have to do with our mode of thinking or our mode of life? We cannot engage with the complexity of this reality without turning our attention to the many layers of abstraction that are present in our daily life, abstractions that exist not just in thought but in the material, practical activity of life.

Abstraction was a central concern of Marx, and it drove the investigations set out in *The German Ideology*. It is crucial, however, to recognize that in the approach of historical materialism laid out in this text, Marx and Engels forcefully articulated the need to not consider abstraction only in processes of thought or as expressed in language. Instead, they argued that we must begin with the material conditions in which we live. Thus, the question of how people engage in abstraction is not simply assumed to be an invention of the mind. It is not our intention to reiterate Marx's analysis of capitalism and its major historical, productive forces. It is sufficient to remind ourselves that the major characteristics of capitalism as a mode of producing and reproducing life involve: 1) separating the majority of human beings from any other means of subsistence than the wage; 2) privatizing access to the means of subsistence through the relations of property; 3) atomizing life into its smallest components and commodifying them; and 4) creating social divisions amongst humans that align their labour with these processes of atomization, commodification and privatization. In other words, capitalism creates a mode of life in which the only way people can access their basic needs is through the market; it has expanded to the point that even our most personal, affective needs can now be fulfilled through commodified, monetized human interactions, and doing so is seen as a form of 'choice', 'autonomy' and 'freedom'. In other words, we live apart from that which we *need* to live: sustenance, shelter, safety and other human beings. In this mode of life, we come to interact with one another through the mechanism of exchange. Our relationships are based on the idea of exchange; when we purchase our cereal we experience the process of exchange as *independent*, and not a reality in which we are utterly *dependent* on other human beings for our basic survival.

This opposition, between how we experience capitalist relations and what they actually are, is an extremely important component of how we think, how we come to know and understand the relations in which we live. Capitalism produces an experiential reality of a fragmented social life. It is impossible for any given individual to experience, for themselves in real time, the complexity or entirety of these relations. They may be physically thousands of miles away from where their food comes from, where their clothes are made, and so on. These relationships are experienced as abstractions in both forms of thought and practical activity. The abstractions can become so generalized that human beings disappear from these processes and relationships entirely; 'systems', 'structures', 'markets' and 'bureaucracies' do the work of organizing our daily life. In this way, 'within the division of labour these relations are bound to acquire independent existence in relation to individuals. All relations can be expressed in language only in the form of concepts. That these general ideas and concepts are looked upon as mysterious forces is the necessary result of the fact that the real relations, of which they are the expression, have acquired independent existence' (Marx and Engels, 1968, p. 406).

Consider, for a moment, some of the concepts of capitalism: commodity, individual, competition. Each of these embodies a central contradiction in capitalist social life; take, for example, the notion of individuals in competition with one another. Within capitalist social relations we are meant to understand ourselves as autonomous individuals, acting through the mechanism of choice, pursuing our own self-interests, maximizing our own happiness, and celebrating our freedom. This narrative is dependent on the idea that we each function highly independently of the social body as we pursue the production and reproduction of our lives. However, as Derek Sayer argued:

> For Marx ... this appearance of individual autonomy, of lack of dependence on social relations, is ultimately illusory. The more the division of labour which individualizes people expands, the more socially interdependent individuals actually become. Given capitalism's inherent dynamism, ultimately such interdependence becomes global, through the world market. Overt relations of personal dependency give way to general objective dependency-relations. (1987, p. 99)

How can we be fully independent beings, when the vast majority of us are unable to meet our daily needs independently? We cannot care for our own bodies without a deeply complex set of social relations to other human beings. However, in our daily lives we do not experience these contradictions *as* contradictions. We do not see these fundamental, material and social relations as part of our reality. Not only is there a contradiction present here, but what we understand as the power of our 'individuality' is also an abstraction. Therefore, our use of the concept of abstraction is to indicate the ripping apart of social forms that are necessarily, dialectically related; this process produces a fragmented, compartmentalized, disembodied ontology and epistemology, hence the violence Marx attributes to this process as an essential characteristic of capitalism. The challenge for revolutionary feminist educators is the task of contending with the complexity of abstraction in which we live.

In order to engage with the totality of capitalist relations, it is imperative we understand abstraction *as* abstraction. It is not just a philosophical trick or way of thinking. It is a *particular* way of thinking that expresses a way of living, and it is a way of thinking that in turn conditions a way of life. For example, following Marx (1992), many Marxist historians, including Ellen Meiksins Wood, E.P. Thompson, Peter Linebaugh, Marcus Rediker, Maria Mies and Silvia Federici have argued that in feudal society, exploitation was more visible and transparent. While Sayer (1987) acknowledges that we could debate the details of this point, particularly in relation to constructs of fealty and reciprocity, it is also the case that under feudalism what was work 'for oneself' and what was work 'for one's lord' were easier to discern. When rulers strayed too far from this norm, peasants revolted. Under the relations of the wage, this separation collapses in daily experience. The material form of labour under capitalism, represented through the wage and embodied in the contradiction between labour and capital, masks the 'social nature of production and the private nature of appropriation' (Hobsbawm, 1973, p. 13). Capitalism, however, is a revolution in the co-operative social relations that produce and reproduce life. These distances and displacements take ontological form as abstraction and epistemological form as ideology.

Without grasping the nature of abstraction in daily life, it is impossible for critical educators, of any stripe, to bring out the materiality of the social relations and forms of our existence. This is because, as Marx argued, 'relations can be expressed ... only in ideas' (Marx, 1993, p. 163), and the kinds of ideas we use to describe and explain this reality are crucial. This is both a theoretical/academic project and a practical one, for every person is constantly using ideas to describe and explain reality, from their interactions on the street to the classroom to the halls of government.

Critical educational theorists have attempted to use the theorization of ideology and consciousness to capture and explain this contradictory set of ontological and epistemological relations. In an article we co-authored with our colleague Genevieve Ritchie, we described the importance of engaging with abstraction and contradiction using a metaphor from our natural world:

Imagine walking along the face of a volcanic rock. In this surface of the earth, a fissure is encountered; the rock has cracked open. While the crack in the surface can be observed in relation to its immediate surroundings (the grain and texture of the rock, the temperature of the air, the winds or tides), these surface appearances do not explain why this fissure has emerged. The rock has cracked because of its own internal pressure; the stress of its own internal force has produced the visible deformation. In order to pry the rock open and understand what has produced this rupture, theory is necessary. Theory, however, can only be built through the continued, unrelenting examination of the rock in relation to its surroundings and its deep essence, what is going on beneath its surface. (Carpenter, Ritchie and Mojab, 2013, p. 7)

To reiterate, battling abstractions found both in the everyday/ everynight social relations of capitalism as well as within bourgeois, ideological forms of knowledge requires ongoing attention to two concurrent processes: first, the actual, existing material relations in which we live; second, the forms of thought that separate us from the materiality of our social and natural worlds, in other words, careful, ongoing and critical reflection on our use of theory and conceptual tools. This careful epistemological consideration is the essence of this book and the project of these collected papers.

We took up this reflection and writing because of serious theoretical concerns about the concepts available to us through the body of theory known as 'critical education'. Take for example the numerous debates concerning what exactly is meant by ideology. Ideology is one of the most ubiquitously used and taken-for-granted concepts in the social sciences. The concept of ideology pre-dates Marx, but his use of it has influenced our thinking for the last 150-plus years. Raymond Williams summarized the various iterations of the term within Marxism as '1) a system of beliefs characteristic of a particular class or group; 2) a system of illusory beliefs – false ideas or false consciousness – which can be contrasted with true and scientific consciousness; 3) the general process of the production of meaning and ideas' (Williams as cited by Bannerji, 2015, p. 164). The concept has been deployed within critical pedagogy to largely refer to 'the production and representation of ideas, values, and beliefs and the manner in which they are expressed and lived out by both individuals and groups' (McLaren, 2003, p. 79). If one examines the proliferation and usage of the concept of ideology in critical education literature, certain questions emerge. These questions reflect some of the inconsistencies Williams pointed to in the quotation above. In many ways, we can see critical educational theory embodying the debates concerning ideology in critical social theory more broadly, but they also demonstrate the ways in which our conceptualization of ideology is bound up with our disciplinary interests. Nevertheless, when examining this body of literature in relation to the problem of abstraction described above, pertinent questions remain.

The first question concerns the relation between the *conceptualization* of ideology and the *description* of how it functions within capitalist social relations. For example, ideology is often described through its function within hegemony, which signals to the reader a reliance on a thread pulled by Anderson (1976) from Gramsci, which is itself a contested interpretation of Gramsci's writing (Thomas, 2010). There is also reliance on Althusser's (1970) arguments concerning how institutions, particularly institutions of the state such as schools, function to reproduce, circulate and enforce particular ideologies. In these critical education usages, ideology is largely understood as systems of ideas that function to legitimate existing power relations, expressed in 'dominant hegemony', and schools are organized by and reproduce these ideologies (Apple, 2004; Anyon, 2011). Borrowing from Donald and Hall's (1985) work, McLaren has argued in multiple places to the effect that ideology includes

> both positive and negative functions. While on the one hand ideology provides us with systems of intelligibility, vocabularies of normalization or standardization, and grammars of design in order to make sense of everyday life, on the other hand such frameworks, grammars, and architectonics of design are always selective, partial, and positional. (2000, p. 103)

According to McLaren, 'all ideas and systems of thought organize a rendition of reality according to their own metaphors, narratives, and rhetoric. There is no "deep structure," totalizing logic, or grand theory pristine in form and innocent in effects which is all together uncontaminated by interest, value or judgement – in short, by ideology' (2003, p. 81). Similarly, Giroux has argued that

> Ideology, as used here, refers to the production, interpretation, and effectivity of meaning. It contains both a positive and negative moment, each of which is determined, in part, by the degree to which it promotes or distorts reflexive thought and action ... I want to argue that three important distinctions provide the foundation for developing a

theory of ideology and classroom practice. First, a distinction must be made between theoretical and practical ideologies ... Theoretical ideologies refer to the beliefs and values embedded in the categories that teachers and students use to shape and interpret the pedagogical process, while practical ideologies refer to the messages and norms embedded in classroom social relations and practices. Second, a distinction must be made between discourse and lived experience as instances of ideology and as the material groundings of ideologies as they are embodied in school 'texts', films, and other cultural artefacts that make up visual and aural media. Third these ideological elements gain their significance only as they are viewed in their articulation with the broader relations of society. (1983, pp. 66–7)

Such attempts as these to articulate ideology through its functionality within classrooms, schools, curricula or media have dominated critical educational theory. When placed in relation to Marx's arguments concerning abstraction and the emergence of idealized forms of social relations, that is, social relations reflected in thought and through concepts, these conceptualizations are unable to push us to understand how and where these ideologies emerge in the first place. What is happening here is a defining of ideology through a description of its functionality, such as through the concept of hegemony, rather than accounting for the role of ideology in mediating the abstractions of life within capitalist social relations. In other words, in this conceptualization, the relation of ideology to ontology is unclear.

This problem leads to a second question about the conceptualization of ideology; specifically, how critical educational theorists have articulated the relation between the emergence of ideology, its form and its content. Both McLaren and Giroux have acknowledged that the concept of ideology involves something about its production. Typically, however, the emergence of ideology is accounted for by several frequently quoted passages from Marx and Engels' *The German Ideology*, exemplified in this argument made by Mayo:

'The ideas of the ruling class are in every epoch the ruling ideas, i.e. the class which is therefore the ruling material force of society, is at the same time its ruling intellectual force.' Marx and Engels go on to argue that 'the ruling ideas are nothing more than the ideal expression of the dominant material relationships, the dominant material relationships grasped as ideas; hence of the relationships which make one class the ruling one, therefore the ideas of its dominance'. Not only does the ruling class produce the ruling ideas, in view of its control over the means of intellectual production, but the dominated classes produce ideas that do not necessarily serve their interests; these classes, that 'lack the means of mental production and are immersed in production relations which they do not control', tend to 'reproduce ideas' that express the dominant material relationships. (2004, p. 38)

This passage is rich in that it encapsulates several of our major concerns. We can see a reduction of the production of ideology to class identity, the ruling class and the dominated class, without an engagement in the notion of class *as a relationship*, or as Marx and Engels articulated 'the ideal expression of the dominant material relationship, the dominant material relationships grasped as ideas' (1968, p. 61). Thus, ideology can be located in a reified iteration of class, expressed in terms of control of mental labour over manual labour, and equated with the interests it serves. Ideology is 'ruling ideas' or ideas that justify and maintain domination. Ideology emerges out of those interests, it enshrines them, protects them, and naturalizes them. What disappears in this articulation is not only the notion of relations, but also human beings themselves. Extending into fetishization, critical education theorists have even imbued ideology with person-like agency, the ability to act independently of human will or even a body and mind. For example, McLaren argued: 'as criticalists surely know, ideology achieves its purpose when it is able to erase evidence of its presence, and often we are aware of its presence only retroactively, when it has exhausted its welcome and is replaced with another offspring' (2005, p. 38). Given such articulations it is no wonder that ideology appears as 'mysterious forces', as Marx and Engels referred to ideas and concepts. What is key here, however, is that this is how ideology *appears*.

Once ideology is given independent status as a concept with agency, it can move freely through theory. This raised another key question for us: How does ideology become a de-politicized, de-radicalized concept in educational theory? The most popular articulations of ideology have only a tangential relation to the class relations described above. For example, drawing from Eagleton, Brookfield argued that ideologies are

'broadly accepted sets of values, beliefs, myths, explanations, and justi-
fications that appear self-evidently true, empirically accurate, personally
relevant, and morally desirable to a majority of the populace, but that
actually work to maintain an unjust social and political order' (2001,
p. 14). The conceptualization of ideology begins to be equated with
beliefs that perpetuate 'injustice', a concept which can be evoked without
having to articulate what exactly is unjust. The most equivocating articulations of ideology within educational theory derive from a reliance on
ideology as 'beliefs'; the idea that ideology should be centrally conceptualized through its form as beliefs or ideas is pervasive across educational
philosophy. Take, for example, a common articulation found in concepts
and keywords texts:

> In Marx's writings, ideologies are world-views that largely
> misrepresent the world as it is. They arise so as to justify the interests
> of the dominant economic group in society ... [In] the broad sense
> of the word, all educators have an 'ideology' since they conduct their
> activities against the background of a view of the world in general and
> of education in particular. (Winch and Gingell, 1999, p. 110)

In this iteration, anyone and everyone has ideology, a formulation that
echoes McLaren's articulation above, drawing from Donald and Hall
(1985) that ideologies are the systems of thought that organize our consciousness and language. Thus, it is possible, according to McLaren, to
create 'oppositional ideologies' which 'attempt to challenge the dominant
ideologies and shatter existing stereotypes' (2003, p. 81). It is here that
we arrive at an irreparable inconsistency in critical educational theory.
The conceptualization of ideologies in this way leads to the imperative
for oppositional ideologies; this conceptualization has not accounted for
the actual complexity of social relations in which we live, and our politics
has been iterated as, Marx and Engels argued, 'combating the phrases of
the world' (1968, p. 30). In this construction, ideology becomes relative;
all classes produce ideology and thus political struggle is primarily about
ideological hegemony rather than revolutionizing relations of production
and reproduction.

This questioning, combined with problems related to the theorization
of race, gender and sexuality, is what led us on a journey to revisit and
explore the conceptual terrain of critical and radical educational theory.

In previous writing, we described the problem of the conceptualization of ideology in this way:

> Ideology is understood here as not just a system of ideas or thought content, but as an epistemology, a way of knowing, that abstracts and fragments social life. Ideological reasoning is accomplished through a complex of tasks that require researchers to disarticulate everyday experience from the conditions and relations in which it takes place. These dismembered bits of human life are then arranged within the framework of pre-existing interpretive notions. The concepts, categories, and theories that result from this process are then given power to frame and interpret other social phenomena. This is the process described by Marx and Engels in *The German Ideology* and elaborated on by Dorothy E. Smith as the ideological practice of social inquiry. Ideological methods of reasoning pull apart the social world. They require that elements be removed from their relations so that they can be theorized as abstract concepts that order our interpretation, our consciousness, of the world around us. Pulling apart the social world is a political project; such fragmentation obscures the relationships between various social phenomena and our experiences of exploitation, oppression, and violence. Ideology becomes our way of making sense of our experiences. Marx and Engels argued that 'if in all ideology men and their circumstances appear upside-down as in a *camera-obscura*, this phenomenon arises just as much from their *historical* life-process as the inversion of objects on the retina does from their *physical* life-process.' The error is not in how we think or interpret our experience; the error is in the process of abstraction, in turning things upside down, in order to make sense of them. The ideological reflex is a direct consequence of the mode of life embodied in capitalism; it thrives on the spatial, temporal, and experiential separation of dialectical contradictions in everyday life. (Carpenter and Mojab, 2011, pp. 10–11)

We wrote these words in the midst of our attempt to understand better the complexity of epistemological and ontological relations within capitalism, including processes of abstraction, their relation to everyday/everynight experience, and thus how knowledge about such relations is produced. What is implicit in this articulation, and should be made explicit, is the recognition that abstraction is a human act of consciousness, an active process of knowledge making, and emerges most intensely from human activity within the abstract relations of capitalism. It reflects abstraction and reproduces it, but it does not have to. We are able to use our consciousness to interrupt this process and to interrogate the problem of abstraction. When we do not, we continue to produce ideological forms of knowledge through ideological modes of reasoning. This is a profound and insidious process and cannot be reduced to the academic mistake of de-contextualizing.

What we see in much of critical educational theory is an ideological conceptualization of ideology. It is abstracted (ruptured from its ontological and epistemological relations), reified (turned from a process into a thing), and fetishized (the thing itself is used to interpret and define social reality). This does not mean that critical educational theory has not described some of the important facets of the relation between education, learning and capitalism. It does, however, mean we have not yet adequately explained these relations in their particular and universal iterations. Further, it does not reflect an ethical and political commitment in which we strongly believe, best articulated by Allman when she argued that:

> It is essential to understand that people engaged in uncritical/reproductive praxis will be extremely susceptible to ideological explanations of reality and that even those who are attempting to engage in critical/revolutionary praxis must be constantly vigilant with respect to ideology. To reiterate, ideology is the seemingly coherent expression of real separations, or fragments, of reality and real inversion in human experience; therefore, because ideological explanations draw upon real aspects of people's experience, those who articulate them have the power to persuade people to accept, or resign themselves to, the ideological portrayal of reality. Moreover, since ideology is not only expressed in words but also often embedded in material forms and human practices, in the absence of continuous critical scrutiny, we all are extremely vulnerable. (2007, p. 65)

Allman not only cautions us to be vigilant in our own use of concepts, but reminds us that the seemingly coherent explanation of reality that is offered through ideological modes of reasoning makes these explanations extremely difficult to combat. In order to address them, we cannot limit our engagement to their content, form or functionality. We must demonstrate how they keep us from understanding, at a deep level, the reality of contradiction in our own experience; our investigations and explanations must depart from and arrive at everyday/everynight relations. They must also be grounded in the actual material and social reality in which we live, including the complexity of abstractions we experience every day. As Allman has argued, this revolutionary praxis is 'aimed at humanising the relation between "knowing" and "being"' (2007, p. 63).

Coming back to revolutionary feminism

> It is necessary to teach by living and speaking those truths, which we believe and know beyond understanding. Because in this way alone we can survive, by taking part in a process of life that is creative and continuing, that is growth. (Lorde, 2007, p. 43)

Critical education and critical theorizations of learning have long contended with the allegation of dogmatism. This is an often-hurled epithet, a way of dismissing any person who utilizes theory or experience to contest the status quo. Those who manoeuvre to protect the powerful or to shore up the totality of social relations of capitalism and their expansion are rarely accused of dogmatism. Their ideas and their actions are assumed to be in the interests of freedom, largely conceived through concepts such as autonomy, choice and rationality. From this standpoint, the theorization of learning looks many different ways, in part because there is a multiplicity of ways in which to do this 'shoring up' work. Not all of it is as explicit as the instrumentalism Freire identified in his banking model critique, in which all agents in the learning relation ('teacher' and 'learner') are commodified and knowledge itself is abstract, reified and ready to take to market. Learning in this frame, which is insidious and wears many masks including the current neoliberal, behaviourist orientation towards competencies and outcomes, is seen solely as a process of acquisition. Much like the accumulating of capital, learning is a deeply privatized process in which learners horde as much knowledge as possible in order to put it into circulation to produce themselves as a valuable commodity, as labour power and human capital. As educators we then concern ourselves with the regulation of this market and deploy our own language of accountability to this process.

What we have argued thus far, and which is also reflected in the chapters in this book, is a commitment to the use of concepts, theories and abstraction *in a particular way*. Bertell Ollman (1993, 2003) has written extensively on Marx's engagement with the problem of abstraction in knowledge production, sentiments which are echoed by Allman and which we have explored in depth throughout Chapters 3 and 4 as well as in other writings (Carpenter and Mojab, 2011; Carpenter, Ritchie and Mojab, 2013). The key concern we raised above, in our discussion of ideology, is the way in which concepts are used in theorizing the social and material reality of capitalism and the processes/relations we call 'learning' and 'education'. The theorization of learning within critical education, drawing largely from research done in the terrains of social movements, activism and community mobilization, embodies a similar conceptual problem to that of the broader field. To use concepts to categorize and describe the phenomenon of learning has been a popular approach to studying processes of radicalization, politicization and conscientization and is taken up in theories such as social movement learning, activist learning, critical consciousness and praxis. When reading this literature, we are struck by its similarities to the subtlety of the critique put forward by Marx and Engels in the course of their debates with idealist socialists. In these debates, Marx and Engels demonstrated that 'though ideology may begin with the real world, it proceeds by constructing a concept or theory that supplants the original and treats original actualities as expressions or effects of the concept or theory' (Smith, 2011, p. 28). Smith points out that Marx and Engels made this critique in part as a self-critique of their early work that began with a given concept, for example 'estrangement', and that they attempted to move away from 'the treatment of concepts as if they were determinants of the "real life" processes in which they originate' (p. 29).

We find that studies of critical learning processes that begin with abstractions such as informal learning, tacit learning, ideology and discourse, experience and learning, and lifelong learning embody this same process of ideology formation, as do feminist pedagogies that rely solely upon culture and language to explore the relations of women's lives (as discussed in Chapter 4). For example, when Foley, in a popular approach to studying social movement activism, advises his readers to begin with questions such as 'what are the ideological and discursive practices and struggles of social movement actors and their opponents? To what extent do these practices and struggles facilitate or hinder emancipatory learning and action?' (1999, p. 10), he directs enquirers to look through particular constructs such as ideology or discourse in order to interpret real practices and directs their attention away from the actual realities and conditions that produce particular forms of social struggle. This is done in the service of naming some learning as emancipatory and identifying the circulation of ideologies and discourses with the assumption that actors with particular forms of consciousness are 'emancipated' or 'radical'. Ultimately, such an analysis reifies consciousness, separates it from praxis, from materiality. This involves analysing a social context for the presence or absence of certain predetermined conceptual indicators of 'critical' learning and ignores the existing social relations, particularly of gender and race, which are also part of the social formation (Gorman, 2002, 2007).

Similar to our unease with the conceptualization of ideology, such conceptualizations of learning and its relation to consciousness and praxis have driven our work. We find much in this body of literature that contradicts our own experiences as educators and activists and which does not engage with the complex, abstracted relations of capitalism in which we live, which we explore in Chapter 2. A very frequent and concerning phenomenon is the articulation of critical consciousness as being composed of particular sets of ideas or patterns of belief, as expressing 'oppositional ideologies'. In this popular, and insidious, conceptualization, critical consciousness is the outcome of replacing systems of thought that are 'ideological' or 'false' with ones that are presumed to be 'critical' or 'radical'. The vast pedagogical implications of these theories have been the foundation of countless experiences in which educators seek to impose their view of reality on their students, ultimately leaving learners with a language of critique but no ability to embody the critical ontologically or extend it beyond its particulars. It is focused on the outcome of analysis rather than analysis itself and in this way is deeply instrumentalist. The absence of a dialectical, materialist and historical conceptualization of consciousness and praxis and an understanding of the epistemological and ontological character of ideology drives these difficulties; much of what is collected in this text is an attempt to understand and engage this phenomenon.

Our own commitment to fully understanding Marx's philosophy of praxis, and Allman's articulation of this philosophy as the central component of a critical educational project, has led us to think deeply about the struggle to become revolutionary subjects who are able to engage with the contradictory, abstracted relations of capitalism, patriarchy and imperialism. This process, as articulated by Allman, is not focused solely on a particular analysis of capitalism or patriarchy. It is focused on the process of humanization, which is 'always a collective, a social, process, perhaps best expressed by conceptualizing our individuality as internally related to our collectivity, to humanity, such that the harmonious, progressive development of one is impossible unless inner-connected to the harmonious progressive development of all' (Allman, 2007, p. 62). This refrain may sound familiar to many, often expressed through references to the ways in which 'your liberation is bound up with mine'. However, Allman was arguing something more complex. In this conceptualization, what we understand as 'learning' involves directly addressing the relation between epistemology and ontology. It is not focused on the content of ideas, on the presence or absence of particular beliefs, but on a process of building knowledge through engagement with the limits of experience and processes of abstraction. Allman argued:

> Rather than relating to knowledge as if it were a thing to be acquired or possessed, with Marx's epistemology, knowledge is a tool that we use to delve deeply into reality, and it is a tool that we constantly test in order to ascertain whether it is enabling us to develop a more complex and comprehensive understanding of the world and our existence and experiences within it. (2007, p. 61)

We would expand Allman's argument by saying that a revolutionary praxis is not only focused on addressing the contradiction between knowing/being in capitalist social relations, but also allows us to move forward into the underlying and driving contradictions in contemporary capitalism, which is in the stage of imperialism, that is, dominated by monopolies and financial capital, and the potential this knowledge holds for undertaking profound radical change, as discussed in Chapter 6. We want to flag briefly here that this text draws upon a theorization of imperialism as a stage in the development of capitalism. There is a great deal of debate concerning the nature of Lenin's articulation of imperialism as the 'highest' or 'latest' stage of capitalist development (for example, see Editor's Notes, *Monthly Review*, January 2004). Here we have developed a line of argument that sees imperialism not as a necessarily last stage of capitalism, but as one that is dominated by the contradictions of finance, monopoly capital.

The implications of this conceptualization apply to feminist theory and pedagogical writing as well. Bannerji argues that Marxist feminists often use Marx's

> critique of ideology, especially the process of its production, rather cursorily, conventionally downgrading his interest in consciousness. This underuse of Marx's interest in consciousness results in ideology being treated as a neutral organization of ideas. Thus in common with non-Marxists, Marxist-feminists also employ ideology as a synonym or a vehicle for political ideas. (2015, p. 170)

Thus, much like critical educational theory, feminist theory has 'not paid much attention to how ideology is created, nor how it is deployed' (p. 171). This 'downgrading' of ideology has resulted in a theorization of learning that weakly conceptualizes the epistemological and ontological relations, the praxis, embodied within the concept, and has instead focused on, again, the phrases of the world and their pedagogical manipulation. For this reason, feminist revolutionary praxis requires not only materializing our understanding of feminism, but also deepening our understanding of the inter-constitutive relations of race and gender that are part of the complex abstractions of life within capitalism. It is our contention that revolutionary feminist praxis can render these relations visible if we adopt a relation to knowing and being that reflects this commitment to knowledge. Through this standpoint,

> inquiry and investigation explore and make explicit and visible what we know only as insiders in and through our practices of knowing. Inquiry here addresses our own practices as knowers. We know them tacitly and in practice; by making them objects of investigation, they are brought into view reflexively as a knowledge not just of the world but of ourselves, of our own doings in it. (Smith, 1990, p. 57)

These invisible relations of patriarchal racist capitalism, so well documented by feminist scholarship, are the experiential reality of an abstracted form of life. Revolutionary feminist praxis must go beyond understanding the expression of these relations, or their affective reality, and move into understanding their emergence and circulation. This orientation towards knowing/being is a form of praxis.

Thus, we have argued (Carpenter and Mojab, 2011) that revolutionary praxis must engage with, and can be facilitated by, engagement with three core contradictions within capitalism. We have expanded on this elsewhere, but we find them important to reiterate. These 'moments' of revolutionary pedagogy offer entry points into conceptualizing processes that can facilitate thinking about how we think. The first, matter and consciousness, directs attention to the knowing/being relation we have discussed in detail here. The second, freedom and necessity, demands attention to the experiential reality of contradictions within capitalism. The third, essence and appearance, begs us to go further into the abstractions and phenomenal forms that we use to 'know' these experiences. The taking up of these moments should be done collectively, from a commitment to revolutionizing humanity over the long-term. We live at a time when the rebellion of women against oppression is spreading internationally and taking on new depths. It is clear that this rebellion can generate explosive power for revolutionary social change. Our deeper understanding of the relationship between abstraction, ideology, history and lived experiences of women can help us to develop a revolutionary feminist learning as one of the key components of global class struggle. Women constitute a sizable labour force in the world, functioning under multi-layered and multiple forms of exploitation and oppression. A revolutionary learning and praxis that can liberate women will surely have the potential to liberate humanity as well.

Forward into the text

The chapters contained herein reflect our struggle to understand revolutionary learning through a dialectical, historical and materialist lens. Each chapter can, if needed, stand on its own, but together they present a growing and creative struggle to revolutionize our thinking around learning and education. Before moving to the chapters, we would like to pause to consider the following passage from noted historians Peter Linebaugh and Marcus Rediker:

> The emphasis in modern labor history on the white, male, skilled, waged, nationalistic, propertied artisan/citizen or industrial worker has hidden the history of the Atlantic proletariat of the seventeenth, eighteenth, and early nineteenth centuries. That the proletariat was not a monster, it was not a unified cultural class, and it was not a race. This class was *anonymous, nameless...* It was *landless, expropriated.* It lost the integument of the commons to cover and protect its needs. It was *poor,* lacking property, money, or material riches of any kind. It was often unwaged, forced to perform the unpaid labor of capitalism. It was often hungry, with uncertain means of survival. It was *mobile, transatlantic.* It powered industries of worldwide transportation. It left the land, migrating from country to town, from region to region, across the oceans, and from one island to another. It was *terrorized, subject to coercion.* Its hide was calloused by indentured labour, galley slavery, plantation slavery, convict transportation, the workhouse, the house of correction. Its origins were often traumatic: enclosure, capture, and imprisonment left lasting marks. It was *female* and *male,* of *all ages.* (Indeed, the very term proletarian originally referred to poor women who served the state by bearing children.) ... It was *multitudinous, numerous,* and *growing.* Whether in a square, at a market, on a common, in a regiment, or on a man-of-war with banners flying and drums beating, its gathering were wondrous to contemporaries. It was *numbered, weighed,* and *measured.* Unknown as individuals or by name, it was objectified and counted for purposes of taxation, production, and reproduction. It was *co-operative* and *labouring.* The collective power of the many rather than the skilled labor of the one produced its most forceful energy. It moved burdens, shifted earth, and transformed the landscape. It was *motley,* both dressed and multiethnic in appearance. Like Caliban, it originated in Europe, Africa, and America. It included clowns, or cloons (i.e., country people). It was without genealogical unity. It was *vulgar.* It spoke its own speech, with a distinctive pronunciation, lexicon, and grammar made up of slang, cant, jargon, and pidgin-talk from work, the street, the prison, the gang, and the dock. It was *planetary,* in its origins, its

motions, and its consciousness. Finally, the proletariat *was self-active, creative*; it was-and is-alive; it is onamove.

What does the experience of this proletariat have to offer us today? (2012, pp. 332–3)

In our Marxist reading group, we found inspiration in this passage. Reading through this analysis we saw in this history the preconditions of many of the realities we face today. We also see an expression of the particularity and universality of both capitalist social relations and the long historical opposition to the consolidation of those relations. This proletariat was, as feminist revolutionary praxis must become, uncompromising (vulgar), global (planetary), bold (self-active, creative), 'alive', and 'onamove'.

References

Allman, P. (1999) *Revolutionary social transformation: Democratic hopes, political possibilities and critical education* (Westport, CT: Bergin & Garvey).

— (2001) *Critical education against global capitalism: Karl Marx and revolutionary critical education* (Westport, CT: Bergin & Garvey).

— (2007) *On Marx: An introduction to the revolutionary intellect of Karl Marx* (Rotterdam: Sense).

Althusser, L. (1970) *Lenin and philosophy and other essays* (London: Monthly Review).

Anderson, P. (1976) 'The antinomies of Antonio Gramsci', *New Left Review*, Vol. 100, 5–78.

Anyon, J. (2011) *Marx and education* (New York: Routledge).

Apple, M. (2004) *Ideology and curriculum* (3rd edn) (New York: Routledge-Falmer).

Au, W. (2007) 'Epistemology of the oppressed: The dialectics of Paulo Freire's theory of knowledge', *Journal for Critical Education Policy Studies*, Vol. 5. Available at http://www.jceps.com/archives/551.

Bannerji, H. (1995) *Thinking through: Essays on feminism, Marxism, and anti-racism* (Toronto: Women's Press).

— (2000) 'Pygmalion nation: Towards a critique of subaltern studies and the "resolution of the women's question"', in H. Bannerji, S. Mojab and J. Whitehead (eds), *Of property and propriety: The role of gender and class in imperialism and nationalism* (Toronto: University of Toronto Press), pp. 34–84.

— (2001) *Inventing subjects: Studies in hegemony, patriarchy, and colonialism* (New Delhi: Tulika).

— (2011) 'Building from Marx: Reflections on "race", gender, and class', in S. Carpenter and S. Mojab (eds), *Educating from Marx: Race, gender, and learning* (New York: Palgrave), pp. 41 60.

— (2015) 'Ideology', in S. Mojab (ed.), *Marxism and Feminism* (London: Zed), pp. 161–80.

— (2016) 'Politics and ideology', *Socialist Studies*, Vol. 11, No. 1, 3–22.

Brookfield, S. (2001) 'Repositioning ideology critique in a critical theory of adult learning', *Adult Education Quarterly*, Vol. 52, No. 7, 7–22.

Carpenter, S. and Mojab, S. (eds) (2011) *Educating from Marx: Race, gender, and learning* (New York: Palgrave).

Carpenter, S., Ritchie, G. and Mojab, S. (2013) 'The dialectics of praxis', *Socialist Studies*, Vol. 9, No. 1, 1–17.

Donald, J., and Hall, S. (eds) (1985) *Politics and ideology* (London: Open University Press).

Foley, G. (1999) *Learning in social action: A contribution to understanding informal education* (London: Zed).

Giroux, H. (1983) *Theory and resistance in education: A pedagogy for the opposition* (South Hadley, MA: Bergin & Garvey).

Giroux, H. and McLaren, P. (eds) (1994) *Between borders: Pedagogy and the politics of cultural studies* (New York: Routledge).

Gorman, R. (2002) 'The limits of "informal learning": Adult education research and the individualizing of political consciousness', in *21st Annual National Conference Proceedings* (Toronto: OISE/UT), pp. 122–27.

— (2007) 'The feminist standpoint and the trouble with "informal learning": A way forwards for Marxist-feminist educational research', in A. Green, G. Rikowski and H. Raduntz (eds), *Renewing dialogues in Marxism and education: Openings* (New York: Palgrave Macmillan), pp. 183–99.

Hobsbawm, E.J. (1973) 'Class consciousness in history', in I. Mészaros (ed.), *Aspects of history and class consciousness* (London: Routledge and Kegan Paul), pp. 5–21.

Linebaugh, P. and Rediker, M. (2012) *The many-headed hydra: The hidden history of the revolutionary Atlantic* (2nd edn) (London: Verso).

Lorde, A. (2007) 'The transformation of silence into language and action', in *Sister outsider* (Berkeley: Cross Press), pp. 40–5.

McDonald, J. and Hall, S. (eds) (1985) *Politics and ideology: A reader* (London: Open University Press).

McLaren, P. (2000) *Che Guevara, Paulo Freire, and the pedagogy of revolution* (Lanham, MD: Rowman & Littlefield).

— (2003) 'Critical pedagogy: A look at the major concepts', in A. Darder, M. Baltodano and R.D. Torres (eds), *The Critical Pedagogy Reader* (New York: RoutledgeFalmer), pp. 69–96.

— (2005) *Capitalists and conquerors: A critical pedagogy against empire* (Lanham, MD: Rowman & Littlefield).

Marx, K. (1986 [1894]) *Capital, Volume 3: The process of capitalist production as a whole* (Moscow: Progress).

— (1992 [1867]) *Capital, Volume 1: A critique of political economy*, trans. B. Fowkes (New York: Penguin).

— (1993 [1858]) *Grundrisse: Foundations of the critique of political economy*, trans. M. Nicolaus (London: Penguin).

Marx, K. and Engels, F. (1968 [1846]) *The German ideology*, trans. S. Ryazanskaya (Moscow: Progress).

Mayo, P. (2004) *Liberating praxis: Paulo Freire's legacy for radical education and politics* (Rotterdam: Sense).

Ollman, B. (1993) *Dialectical investigations* (New York: Routledge).

— (2003) *Dance of the dialectic: Steps in Marx's method* (Urbana: University of Illinois Press).

Sayer, D. (1987) *The violence of abstraction: The analytical foundations of historical materialism* (New York: Basil Blackwell).

Smith, D. (1988) *The everyday world as problematic* (Toronto: University of Toronto Press).

— (1990) *The conceptual practices of power: A feminist sociology of knowledge* (Boston: Northeastern University Press).

— (1999) *Writing the social: Critique, theory, and investigations* (Toronto: University of Toronto Press).

— (2011) 'Ideology, science and social relations: A reinterpretation of Marx's epistemology', in S. Carpenter and S. Mojab (eds), *Educating from Marx: Race, gender, and learning* (New York: Palgrave), pp. 19–40.

Thomas, P. (2010) *The Gramscian moment: Philosophy, hegemony, and Marxism* (Chicago: Haymarket).

Winch, C. and Gingell, J. (1999) *Key concepts in the philosophy of education* (London: Routledge).

2

What is 'Critical' About
Critical Educational Theory?

Before moving into a more substantial theoretical discussion of revolutionary learning, we want to situate ourselves in the broader field of critical educational theory by clearly articulating the key points of departure of our work. In this chapter, we propose a new approach to a survey of the field of critical educational theory; rather than describing it we aim to interrogate it. We do not intend to repeat what has been done successfully elsewhere, which has provided extensive literature reviews, historical summations, mappings of the field and summaries of the debates and trends (Brookfield and Holst, 2011; Coben, 1998; Collins, 2006; Foley, 1999; Holst, 2002; Jones, 2011; Lovett, 1988; McLaren, 2000, 2005; McLaren and Leonard, 1993; Macrine, McLaren and Hill, 2010; Mayo, 1999, 2004; Newman, 1994, 2006; Rikowksi, 1996, 1997; Thompson, 1980, 1982, 1997; Wangoola and Youngman, 1996; Youngman, 1986, 2000). Instead, we propose a debate around a universal question that is applicable to critical educators of diverse theoretical and political persuasions: What does it mean to be 'critical' in our historical moment? The title of this chapter reflects this basic but under-explored problematic at the centre of educational theorization and practice, which has been the subject of an ongoing debate (Brookfield, 2003; McLaren and Jaramillo, 2010; Moraes, 2003).

The question of 'what is critical about critical education' has emerged from our teaching and research in and outside of North America. In our courses we frequently observe a deeply humanist, passionate and emotional response from students as we explore the myriad of social conditions and problems of injustice faced by people the world over. They are deeply unsettled by the social, cultural, economic and ecological state of the world. However, their modes of analysis are often fractured, eclectic and in contradiction with one another as their attentions are pulled in competing directions by incomplete theoretical explanations. They are often left with a tenuous ability to understand social relations, including their own lives, as the result of dynamic contradictions in our social, cultural and material world. This has deep implications for their political imagination. What we see at the centre of this confusion are theorizations of notions of social change and social justice that leave obscured the history and the practices behind these notions. Ideas for social change have a history to them, and that history tells us much about the assumptions that drive them and the limitations of their impact and scope. Educators and learners sometimes miss this important history and process of theorization in their genuine desire to make the world a better place, a desire complicated by questions about inequality, identity, positionality and social justice. They can 'hunt assumptions', as Brookfield (1995, p. 2) has argued is at the centre for critical thought, but they cannot find where the assumptions came from in the first place. In other words, they do not understand their contemporary conditions as the historical result of certain preconditions.

As educators and scholars, this problem compels us to go deeper into the notion of 'being critical'. There are many useful tools in this exploration, particularly the extension of dialectical analysis into feminism, anti-racism, social change and resistance, education and learning, and the construction of knowledge (Allman, 1999, 2001, 2007; Au, 2006, 2007a, 2007b; Bannerji, 1995, 2011; Ebert, 1996, 2009; Federici, 2004; Harvey, 2010; Holst, 1999, 2002; Mies, 1986; Ollman, 2003; Sayer, 1987; Smith, 1990, 2011). However, there are also bodies of theory that provide a partial analysis or, at best, make unobservable contradictions observable. Specifically, we have noticed particular trends in our classrooms. First, we often see a resistance to critical theorization based on assumptions about Marxism as being mechanical and deterministic. Second, the horizons of innovative forms of resistance appear wrapped up in either social-democratic romanticizations of participation or leaderless mobilizations that celebrate their lack of organization. Third, we also work against a nihilistic humanism that draws learners into a survivalist mentality that prioritizes the self over the social and emphasizes critical introspection. Finally, we have a body of feminist, anti-racist and post-colonial literature that is profoundly important to critical scholarship, but which is predominantly locked in abstracted frames of culture and which lacks a strong grounding in the materiality of social relations. For example, Butler (2006) makes a similar argument when she explores theorizations of identity and difference in the context of post-9/11 militarism and imperialism.

We have organized this chapter in such a way as to exemplify our critique of and our approach to interrogating the notions of 'critical' embedded in critical educational theory. We begin by more fully explaining our own positions and commitments so as to clarify why we see the way we see. We then explore different articulations of what 'being critical' can mean, with an emphasis on the specificity of historical materialist critique. We conclude with a proposal to reground critical education through attention to three immediate historical tensions in our work as educators. We identify these tensions as: emphasizing class as a structure or identity rather than process or relation; conceptual slippages between neoliberalism and capitalism; and the necessity of theorizing the relation between neoliberalism and imperialism.

Our lens, briefly stated

We identify ourselves intellectually and politically as Marxists and anti-racist feminists and have often written under the category 'Marxist feminism'. We have been engaged, for many years, in the cultivation of a Marxist feminist framework for the field of adult education (Carpenter and Mojab, 2011). While there are many combinations of Marxism and feminism, for us these concepts refer to an intellectual and political position that aims to cultivate feminist and anti-racist dialectical historical materialist analysis and revolutionary praxis. We identify as educators who believe scholarship and teaching to be forms of activism. Thus, the litmus test for theoretical positions are the dictates of their political imaginations and the analytical tools they offer to address the real, contradictory social relations of exploitation and violence that are present in everyday life. What kind of theory helps us to explain the world around us? What kinds of explanations do they offer? What kind of world do they help us to imagine and realize?

For that reason, we draw from readings of feminism, post-colonialism and anti-racism that emphasize dialectical, historical and materialist analysis. At the same time, we read original texts and draw from scholarship on Marx that is historical and dialectical, that focuses on the unity of ontology and epistemology. We also seek out literature that rejects economist, deterministic and mechanical readings of Marx and instead emphasizes the conceptualization of a dialectical understanding of social relations of oppression and exploitation. The unifying feature here is an emphasis on dialectics. Said as simply as possible, dialectics is *a way of thinking* about social life as relationships in which social phenomenon are not abstracted, separated or fragmented from one another (Ollman, 2003). For us, to say that something is understood dialectically is to see it through the lens of its historical emergence, to see the way in which it appears in daily life, and to seek out an explanation of why it appears the way it does in order to understand the essence of the contradictions that form social phenomena. This is a departure from other deployments of the concept of dialectics in critical pedagogical theory, deployments that lack a historical materialist elaboration of this concept (Hernandez, 1997). For example, many educators approach democracy as a philosophy or a set of ideas and ideals. To understand democracy dialectically, one must examine it as a way of organizing social life that emerged historically in tandem with the concentration of capitalist development in Western Europe and North America. It is a historically particular mode of political organization that ensures the basic premises of capitalist life, including private property, individual freedom, competition, the rule of law and civil rights. In its appearance, democracy is representative government run 'by the people'. In its essence, it is the right to inequality. This dialectical mode of analysis reveals the limits of bourgeois democracy, and it tells us that the promise of democracy articulated in the notion of equal rights or equality before the law is indeed *not* universal. This universality shatters into pieces when it encounters social constructs such as race, gender, class, sexuality or indigeneity. In marshalling arguments for rights and democracy to respond to the desires, demands and grievances of social groups, advocates become trapped by ideological categories that not only create conditions of inequality, but are in fact presupposed by relations of inequality, particularly relations of private property and social divisions of labour (Carpenter, 2011; Marx, 1970; Wood, 1995).

It is our claim that dialectics should sit at the centre of any articulation of 'being critical' in social theory. Dialectical thinking, which has a long and varied history of emergence itself, is a form of revolutionary consciousness (Allman, 1999). Ollman argues:

It is revolutionary because it helps us to see the present as a moment through which our society is passing, because it forces us to examine where it has come from and where it is heading as part of learning what it is and because it enables us to grasp that as agents as well as victims in this process, in which everyone and everything is connected, we have the power to affect it. (2003, p. 20)

This is the guiding assumption that provokes our entrance into a debate about what is 'critical' about critical adult education. However, it is important to flesh out some of the implications of the assertion that there are different ways of being critical by explicating how processes of critique are used in pursuit of social change.

Critique versus 'being critical'

A guiding thread to this discussion is a preoccupation with the following question: What do we mean by 'critical?' This question then begs the further question in our title: What is 'critical' about critical education? In an attempt to 'be critical', we face two obstacles that derail our focus on the complexity of social relations and contradiction. On the one hand, 'being critical' is undermined by demands for action, for practice, for possibility, and even for the rejection of theory. On the other hand, 'being critical' is undermined by problems inherent to the notion of critique, which forms the central intellectual practice of 'being critical'. For this reason, we propose that it is very important for educators to be *critical of being critical*. In other words, we must be rigorous in what we mean by the concept 'critical'. Angela Davis has developed a similar argument for a parallel and persistent problem in feminist theory:

The feminist critical impulse, if we take it seriously, involves a dual commitment: a commitment to use knowledge in a transformative way, and to use knowledge to remake the world so that it is better for its inhabitants – not only for human beings, for all its living inhabitants. This commitment entails an obstinate refusal to attribute permanency to that which exists in the present, simply because it exists. This commitment simultaneously drives us to examine the conceptual and organizing tools we use, not to take them for granted. (2008, pp. 20–1)

We believe that a similar commitment drives those who identify as critical educators. For this reason, a continued commitment to the critical examination of our conceptual tools is of the utmost importance.

The word 'critical' is often used as a catch-all term to denote some form of opposition to the mainstream, the status quo, or 'being liberal'. For example, we have critical education, critical race theory, critical feminism and critical social theories. But we should ask two important questions: What are we being critical of, *and* how are we doing it? To be critical implies that one is engaging in a process of critique. However, not all critiques assume to perform the same function or result in explanations that are politically useful in the same ways. What we mean by this is that the process of critique itself is not neutral.

We can say, broadly, as Teresa Ebert (1996) has done, that there are at least two different types of critique popular in the social sciences today. She argued that one is *immanent critique*, dynamically seen in the process of deconstruction. In this process, we take apart the construction of a particular social formation. Deconstruction often begins by demonstrating that human relations are social to begin with, and not a natural by-product of human life. A classic example of this is the construction of 'race', which only the most conservative of thinkers still asserts is biological in origin. We have used quotation marks around this category to refer to our contestation of its construction and deployment; specifically, the notion that 'race' is separate and autonomous from social relations. Many agree that 'race' is a historical and social construction used to organize human relations and systems of power. It is not a genetic 'thing'. Once this is established, we can then engage in processes of critique that demonstrate just how pervasive and insidious the problem of racism is in contemporary life and how it operates, largely through language, representation and meaning systems. For instance, we can research how racialization operates in classrooms, how it influences assumptions about teaching and learning, and how it mitigates experiences in educational institutions.

Ebert (1996) argues that there is another kind of critique that is embodied in the notion of *critique-al*, or rather, historical materialist critique. In this form of critique, social formations are located in social relations of production and reproduction. Their historical specificity and operation is demonstrated in relation to complex webs of social relations, forms of consciousness, organizations of human labour and operations of ideology. This does not mean attributing everything to capitalism; it means identifying the social organization of historical phenomena, their root in forms of human labour, social organization and consciousness.

To explain the different forms of critique to students, we often use the language of *describing a social problem* versus *explaining the social problem*. One form of 'being critical' describes the contours and realities of our conditions. It highlights elements of social life that are otherwise unobservable. This descriptive process is extremely useful to those who are unable to see the world from the standpoint of others or to recognize, without the force of evidence, that not everyone experiences the world as they do. It is also necessary to the process of explanation, but alone it is insufficient.

For still others, to be critical is to question the pretences of power, to speak truth to its origins, and you are thus an agitator or, if you are lucky, a shit stirrer. This is the kind of critique that we hope is driven by a desire to explain why we live the way we live in such a way that our social life becomes an object of contestation. As human beings, we choose, within history, to live amongst and with each other and our natural world in particular ways. This form of 'being critical', embodied in historical materialist critique, should lead us to revolutionize our relations *in their entirety*. In a complex and dynamic way, this project has remained at the centre of critical education scholarship and practice for more than a century.

Given these debates, students and scholars of education should ask important questions. What kind of critique does critical education offer us? And of what use is it? It is our position that 'critical' education should not simply describe the world as it is. It should not take as its main pedagogical purpose the pointing out of this reality to those for whom this 'critical' vision is obscured. Rather, 'critical' education should explain the source, function, expression and operation of the contradictions that constitute our social relations. As Ollman has argued,

> With dialectics we are made to question what kind of changes are already occurring and what kind of changes are possible. The dialectic is revolutionary, as [Bertolt] Brecht points out, because it helps us to pose such questions in a manner that makes effective action possible ... The dialectic is critical because it helps us to become critical of what our role has been up to now. (2003, p. 20)

It is our position that critical education should equip learners with the tools of social analysis to continue this explanation on their own and translate this analysis into mobilization, resistance and revolution.

This perspective leads us to read the terrain of critical education in particular ways. Most importantly, it requires us to *historicize* and *materialize* the field. This means understanding the development of critical education as part of the history of ideas and social movements – which come into existence through their relationships to one another – and their relationship to the material and social organization of daily life.

Seeing history in critical education

The histories of critical education are indivisible from larger processes in global history, particularly the development of Marxist and critical forms of social theory and the history of social movements, mobilizations and revolutionary struggles. These histories are long, fractured, diverse and subject to multiple interpretations. They are also not separate histories, but deeply entwined and informative of each other. A detailed discussion of the relationship between Marxist and critical social theory and revolutionary human practice is far beyond the scope of this chapter. However, educators have both appeared and inserted themselves into this history at different and important points. When we examine global history from the standpoint of education, we see the emergence of certain trends or salient ideas at particular historical moments. These trends do not disappear; rather, they evolve and change with time into definite areas within the critical education tradition.

For example, we can imagine a world characterized by two world wars and the Great Depression, the failure of industrial capitalism to meet the needs of the working masses of North America and Western Europe, and ongoing imperialist expansion and rivalry. In this context of great deprivation, political unrest, and reform in social policy, adult education emerged with large-scale projects focused on supporting and developing trade-union activity and the development of localized alternatives to economic organization, particularly in the form of social and economic co-operatives. Two of the great adult education projects of North America, the Antigonish movement (Welton, 2001) and the Highlander Folk School (Horton, 1990), emerged out of this context, a context that included numerous socialist schools associated with political organization and trade-union movements.

In the 1950s and 1960s, educators faced the challenges of a world characterized by the widespread resistance of colonized and enslaved peoples against their subordination to imperialism and white supremacy. This era contained a critique of dominant Marxist traditions through decades of work on the knowledges of colonized peoples, resulting in critical anti-colonial educational projects and revolutionary struggles embodied in the work of Fanon (2005), Freire (1970), Guevara (Holst, 2009; Löwy, 1973), DuBois (DuBois, 1968; Guy, 2009), Boggs (1998), Jones (Davies, 2008) and Cabral (Chabal, 1983). By the late 1960s, the revolutionary critique offered by these authors deeply influenced North American and European educators, who worked to craft literacy, political, cultural and economic education programmes that unsettled the normalization of white-settler nations.

It is extremely important that critical educators not bypass the significance of the socialist experiments in the USSR and China, in particular during the early years of these burgeoning communist states. For example, whereas widespread literacy campaigns throughout North America were organized in the service of colonial expansion (Walter, 2003), the influence of adult and popular education programmes in China and the USSR gave rise to later socialist and populist projects in Africa, Southeast Asia, the Middle East and Latin America (Carnoy and Samoff, 1990). These included literacy campaigns, but also land and agrarian reform, public health, housing, decolonization, anti-apartheid and anti-militarism. This history is clearly evidenced in the International Council of Adult Education documentation and its journal *Convergence/ Convergencia*.

This 'critical' left history was deeply influential on and influenced by the ongoing struggles of international feminist movements. Feminist critiques of social organization and their visions of resistance to subordination and domination emerged concurrently with anti-colonial and anti-capitalist work, particularly the ongoing critique of the social relations of reproduction. Socialist feminist educators worked to develop spaces where women could collectively articulate the conditions of violence and subordination that characterize the universal relations of patriarchy in local contexts, resulting in extensive reform of patriarchal social relations (Dalla Costa and James, 1975; Hart, 1992; James, 2012;

Maguire, 1987; Thompson, 1982, 1983). Feminist education projects, ranging from consciousness-raising groups to feminist pedagogy projects in schools, emerged on a global scale.

Through the standpoint of educators, we enter into the 'beginning' of our current crises, the emergence of neoliberal social policy and the closing down of traditional structures of opposition to capitalist expansion and entrenchment. The impact of the neoliberal environment on critical education cannot be underestimated and partially describes our current moment in which educators find themselves defending the spaces for critical learning, which were established over many years of struggle. In these spaces new social movements have emerged, which then provoke the study of how a fractured left organizes its resistance around objects other than the defeat of capitalist social relations, particularly in an intellectual and political context in which 'there is no alternative' to capitalism (Hall and Turray, 2006). One of the key hallmarks of this era has been a movement by critical educators away from Marx and revolutionary projects and towards critical theory, the Frankfurt School, cultural studies and culturalist readings of Gramsci (Allman and Wallis, 1995), and, particularly in Canada, towards Habermas and his vision of a decolonized lifeworld (Welton, 1995). An important feature of this work is a de-coupling of radical politics from a revolutionary critique of capitalist social relations (McLaren and Jaramillo, 2010) and from the political debates surrounding the emergence of critical pedagogy and resistance theory in relation to formal schooling as well as the cultural turn within these bodies of theory (Rikowski, 1996). These approaches have reduced the politics of critical adult education to a social-democratic critique aimed at the reform, not negation, of capitalist social relations.

Stymied by an environment in which resistance to oppression is largely seen as a matter of trading discourses of subordination for discourses of liberation, a reclamation of the self and identity, some critical educators have launched a return to rigorous and dialectical critiques of capitalist social relations and forms of consciousness (see Chapters 2 and 7 specifically) (Allman, 1999, 2001, 2007; Au, 2007a, 2007b; Colley, 2002; Holst, 2002; Rikowski, 2001). This return involves a re-visioning of advances in socialist, feminist, anti-racist critical pedagogy and theory. The historicization of critical adult education in this chapter demonstrates to us that the emergence of our modes of thought have some social reality behind them. Our assumptions and proposals for critical adult education come from this history, extend this history, move through this history. We arrive, as educators, at a historical moment in which not only are capitalist social relations entrenched and sophisticated, but our attempts to undermine them are complicated by analysis and critique that ignores these historical currents and bedrocks.

Capitalism and the terrains of criticality

Marx's explanation of capitalism, his theory of consciousness (praxis) and the possibility of critical/revolutionary praxis, when taken together, strongly suggest that authentic revolution requires the simultaneous and complementary transformation of both self and society. Neither critical/revolutionary praxis nor authentic revolution can be imposed on people; both must be chosen on the basis of a critical understanding of capitalism and a deeply integrated desire to begin the process of shaping our own and thus humanity's future, or as Antonio Gramsci so aptly put it, on the basis of '...the intellectual base [being] so well rooted, assimilated and experienced that it becomes passion...' (Allman, 2007, p. 34).

We began this chapter with a reflection on the difficulties we face in our classrooms: passionate interest from our students, clouded by social analysis that creates deeper frustrations, an 'analysis towards paralysis' rather than one revealing the internal relations of hetero-patriarchal, imperialist capitalism. Such confusion is often mistaken as a celebration of the complexity and diversity of the world they live in, instead of a set of theoretical ideas that ultimately re-entrench the status quo. Our students struggle to unlock the contradictions they see around them and to recognize the tensions that exist behind surface appearances. They latch onto the explanatory frameworks that are most immediate to them, such as the notions of power/privilege and intersectionality/positionality, rather than connecting these ideas to the deeper, inner relations in our mode of social life.

Given the events of the past 15 years, particularly since 9/11, the necessity of a critical education that emerges from historical materialist critique is more apparent now than it has been for the last three decades. Daily life today is characterized by the overwhelming problems of war, militarism, incarceration, terror, poverty, hunger, ecological catastrophe, state violence and a deeply entrenched public bewilderment as to how to understand and address these problems. In this context, dialectical and historical materialist critique directs our attention to problems in the theory we use to explain these conditions. While we have argued that immanent and social-democratic critique produce unfinished analyses, scholarship that is closer to the historical materialist critique could erroneously perform this function as well. In our observation, there are three tendencies or slippages through which this happens in critical education research and practice.

First, Marxist scholarship has for too long focused on the question of class instead of social and material relations. It has focused on productive labour at the expense of reproductive labour. It has worked from a static, mechanical notion of class rather than understanding class as a relation between people who are socially organized as gendered, sexed and raced bodies (Rikowski, 2001). Critical education scholarship has reproduced this mistake and continues to do so through a marginaliza-tion and/or tokenization of feminist and anti-racist analysis or through the detachment of gender and race from materiality and class. Critical educators must develop modes of analysis and research agendas that explore the dialectical relations between social identity, social relations and material forces.

Second, critical scholarship, across all disciplines, is preoccupied with the question of neoliberalism. Neoliberalism has been, for the last decade, the panacea of social theory; it is the category used to explain and resolve all social problems and ills. In education, the critique of neoliberalism has entered every domain of scholarship within the field. However, in our own studies of democracy promotion projects in North America and the Middle East (see Chapter 7), we have observed that a reliance on neoliberalism meets its limits when we try to explain why it has emerged in this historical moment. Why so much demand for free markets? Why so much effort into cultivating a neoliberal subject? Is it because rich people are greedy, or, worse, that all people are 'naturally' corrupt? Is it because the state has made the mistake of treating corporations as people? We would argue no. The answer to this question can only be found in a historical materialist understanding of neoliber-alism, an understanding that examines its development as part of the ongoing expansion and concentration of capitalism and as a historically specific response to endemic crisis within capitalism. In other words, an understanding of neoliberalism is incomplete without an understanding of imperialism or the monopoly of finance capital (Harvey, 2003; Mojab, 2011; Wood, 2003).

Third, the emphasis on neoliberalism without imperialism is directly related to the political horizon of critical education. This horizon is unclear. Neoliberalism did not come to dominate the world *spontaneously* through the invisible hand of the market. While its rise was certainly embedded in the dynamics of capitalism, the diffusion of neoliberalism since the 1970s has been achieved through the intervention of the state and the financial organs of the imperialist system such as the World Bank, the World Trade Organization, and the International Monetary Fund. Contrary to the claims of Negri and Hardt in their *Empire* (2000) and *Multitude* (2004), the experience of the last decade reveals not the withering away of the state but, rather, the crucial role of the state in organizing the market-centred world of neoliberalism as well as the launch of unceasing inter-state and regional wars. The role of the state in expanding capital and in the surveillance of resistance is even more decisive. Unorganized, leaderless, de-centred and spontaneous movements of protest cannot force the state–market bloc into sharing wealth with the 'multitude' (on spontaneity, see Chapter 2; for an expanded critique of imperialism see Chapter 6). We would argue that without careful reflection, critical educators could unintentionally bypass an exceedingly important debate and fall subject to a theoretical pull towards reformism. The debates surrounding the Occupy Movement, student mobilizations in Canada and around the world, protests against austerity, and people's rising up against autocratic regimes raise questions about the limits of reformism and its relation to the suppression of revolutionary consciousness. The transition from the current state of affairs to a society without exploitation and oppression is possible, though not without revolutionary consciousness and the exercise of state power for the purpose of creating a society that is radically different from what we have had so far. What is of the utmost importance is that adult educators engage in this debate; that we explore and seriously consider the relationship between our scholarship and the political imaginaries we propose.

Let us end by returning to a theme that has run through this discussion: passion. The passion we see in our classes and amongst our colleagues is for genuine human emancipation. Educators often express an affinity for the *critical humanism* of the critical tradition, but even this *critical humanism* is indefinite in its expression of a vision of emancipation. So let us take a step towards defining what is 'critical' about critical education by expressing fully a vision of what this humanist vocation of education might mean.

> For Marx, the process of humanization, i.e., of becoming more fully human, is always a collective, a social process, perhaps best expressed by conceptualizing our individuality as internally related to our collectivity, to humanity, such that the harmonious, progressive development of one is impossible unless inner-connected to the harmonious progressive development of all. (Allman, 2007, p. 62)

The terrain of criticality in education must be many things at once: historical, dialectical, feminist and anti-racist, but also social, collective and based always in the goal of revolutionary praxis.

References

Allman, P. (1999) *Revolutionary social transformation: Democratic hopes, political possibilities and critical education* (Westport, CT: Bergin & Garvey).

— (2001) *Critical education against global capitalism: Karl Marx and revolutionary critical education* (New York: Greenwood).

— (2007) *On Marx: An introduction to the revolutionary intellect of Karl Marx* (Rotterdam: Sense).

Allman, P. and Wallis, J. (1995) 'Gramsci's challenge to the politics of the left in our times', *International Journal of Lifelong Education*, Vol. 14, No. 2, 120–43.

Au, W. (2006) 'Against economic determinism: Revisiting the roots of neo-Marxism in critical educational theory', *Journal of Critical Education Policy Studies*, Vol. 4, No. 2. Available at http://www.jceps.com/archives/520.

— (2007a) 'Epistemology of the oppressed: The dialectics of Paulo Freire's theory of knowledge', *Journal of Critical Education Policy Studies*, Vol. 5, No. 2. Available at http://www.jceps.com/archives/551.

— (2007b) 'Vygotsky and Lenin on learning: The parallel structures of individual and social development', *Science & Society*, Vol. 71, No. 3, 273–98.

Bannerji, H. (1995) *Thinking through: Essays on feminism, Marxism and anti-racism* (Toronto: Women's Press).

— (2011) 'Building from Marx: Reflections on "race", gender, and class', in S. Carpenter and S. Mojab (eds), *Educating from Marx: Race, gender, and learning* (New York: Palgrave Macmillan), pp. 41–62.

Boggs, G.L. (1998) *Living for change: An autobiography* (Minneapolis: University of Minnesota Press).

Brookfield, S. (1995) *Become a critically reflective teacher* (San Francisco: Jossey-Bass).

— (2003) 'Putting the critical back into critical pedagogy: A commentary on the path of dissent', *Journal of Transformative Education*, Vol. 1, No. 2, 141–9.

Brookfield, S. and Holst, J. (2011) *Radicalizing learning: Adult education for a just world* (San Francisco: Jossey-Bass).

Butler, J. (2006) *Precarious life: The powers of mourning and violence* (London: Verso).

Carnoy, M., and Samoff, J. (1990) *Education and social transition in the Third World* (Princeton: Princeton University Press).

Carpenter, S. (2011) 'Examining the social relations of learning citizenship: Citizenship and ideology in adult education', in S. Carpenter and S. Mojab (eds), *Educating from Marx: Race, gender, and learning* (New York: Palgrave Macmillan), pp. 63–86.

Carpenter, S. and Mojab, S. (eds) (2011) *Educating from Marx: Race, gender, and learning* (New York: Palgrave Macmillan).

Chabal, P. (1983) *Amilcar Cabral: Revolutionary leadership and people's war* (New York: CUP Archive).

Coben, D. (1998) *Radical heroes: Gramsci, Freire and the politics of adult education* (London: Taylor & Francis).

Colley, H. (2002) 'A rough guide to the history of mentoring from a Marxist feminist perspective', *Journal of Education for Teaching*, Vol. 28, 257–73.

Collins, M. (2006) 'The critical legacy: Adult education against the claims of capital', in T. Fenwick, T. Nesbit and B. Spencer (eds), *Contexts of Adult Education: Canadian Perspectives* (Toronto: Thompson Educational), pp. 118–27.

Dalla Costa, M. and James, S. (1975) *The power of women and the subversion of the community* (Bristol: Falling Wall Press).

Davies, C.B. (2008) *Left of Karl Marx: The political life of Black communist Claudia Jones* (Durham: Duke University Press).

Davis, A. (2008) 'A vocabulary for feminist praxis: On war and radical critique', in R. Riley, C. Mohanty and M. Bruce Pratt (eds), *Feminism and war: Confronting US imperialism* (London: Zed), pp. 19–27.

DuBois, W. (1968) *Dusk of dawn: An essay toward an autobiography of a race concept* (New York: Transaction).

Ebert, T.L. (1996) *Ludic feminism and after: Postmodernism, desire, and labor in late capitalism* (Ann Arbor: University of Michigan Press).

— (2009) *The task of cultural critique* (Champaign-Urbana: University of Illinois Press).

Fanon, F. (2005 [1963]) *The wretched of the earth* (New York: Grove).

Federici, S. (2004) *Caliban and the witch: Women, the body and primitive accumulation* (New York: Autonomedia).

Foley, G. (1999) *Learning in social action: a contribution to understanding informal education* (London: Zed).

Freire, P. (1970) *Pedagogy of the oppressed: 30th Anniversary Edition* (New York: Continuum).

Guy, T.C. (2009) 'Selectivity, historical memory and truth: Majoritarian stories and the construction of adult education knowledge', Standing Conference on University Teaching and Research in the Education of Adults (SCUTREA), University of Cambridge, Conference Proceedings, Vol. 39, 200–5.

Hall, B. and Turray, T. (2006) *A review of the state of the field of adult learning: Social movement learning* (Ottawa: Canadian Council on Learning).

Hardt, M. and Negri, A. (2000) *Empire* (Cambridge, MA: Harvard University Press).

— (2004) *Multitude: War and democracy in the age of empire* (New York: Penguin).

Hart, M.U. (1992) *Working and education for life: Feminist and international perspectives on adult education* (New York: Routledge).

Harvey, D. (2003) *The new imperialism* (Oxford: Oxford University Press).

— (2010) *A companion to Marx's Capital Volume 1* (London: Verso).

Hernandez, A. (1997) *Pedagogy, democracy, and feminism: Rethinking the public sphere* (Albany: SUNY Press).

Holst, J.D. (1999) 'The affinities of Lenin and Gramsci: Implications for radical adult education theory and practice', *International Journal of Lifelong Education*, Vol. 18, No. 5, 407–21.

— (2002) *Social movements, civil society, and radical adult education* (New York: Bergin & Garvey).

— (2009) 'The pedagogy of Ernesto Che Guevara', *International Journal of Lifelong Education*, Vol. 28, No. 2, 149–73.

Horton, M. (1990) *The long haul: An autobiography* (New York: Teachers College Press).

James, S. (2012) *Sex, race and class – the perspective of winning. A selection of writings 1952–2011* (Oakland: PM Press).

Jones, P. (ed.) (2011) *Marxism and education: Renewing the dialogue, pedagogy, and culture* (New York: Palgrave Macmillan).

Lovett, T. (ed.) (1988) *Radical approaches to adult education: A reader* (London: Routledge).

Löwy, M. (1973) *The Marxism of Che Guevara: Philosophy, economics, revolutionary warfare* (New York: Rowman & Littlefield).

McLaren, P. (2000) *Che Guevara, Paulo Freire, and the pedagogy of revolution* (New York: Rowman & Littlefield).

McLaren, P. and Jaramillo, N.E. (2010) 'Not neo-Marxist, not post-Marxist, not Marxian, not autonomist Marxism: Reflections on a revolutionary (Marxist) critical pedagogy', *Cultural Studies ↔ Critical Methodologies*, Vol. 10, No. 3, 251–62.

McLaren, P. and Leonard, P. (eds) (1993) *Paulo Freire: A critical encounter* (New York: Routledge).

Macrine, S., McLaren, P. and Hill, D. (eds) (2010) *Revolutionizing pedagogy: Education for social justice within and beyond global neo-liberalism* (New York: Palgrave Macmillan).

Maguire, P. (1987) *Doing participatory research: A feminist approach* (Amherst: University of Massachusetts).

Marx, K. (1970 [1875]) 'Critique of the Gotha programme', *Marx–Engels Selected Works* (MESW), Vol. 3 (Moscow: Progress), pp. 13–30.

Mayo, P. (1999) *Gramsci, Freire and adult education: Possibilities for transformative action* (New York: Palgrave Macmillan).

— (2004) *Liberating praxis: Paulo Freire's legacy for radical education and politics* (Westport, CT: Greenwood).

Mies, M. (1986) *Patriarchy and accumulation on a world scale: Women in the international division of labour* (New York: Palgrave Macmillan).

Mojab, S. (2011) 'Adult education in/and imperialism', in S. Carpenter and S. Mojab (eds), *Educating from Marx: Race, gender, and learning* (New York: Palgrave Macmillan), pp. 167–90.

Moraes, M. (2003) 'The path of dissent: An interview with Peter McLaren', *Journal of Transformative Education*, Vol. 1, No. 2, 117–34.

Nesbit, T. (ed.) (2005) *Class concerns: Adult education and social class* (San Francisco: Jossey-Bass).

Newman, M. (1994) *Defining the enemy: Adult education and social action* (Sydney: Stewart Victor).

— (2006) *Teaching defiance: Stories and strategies for activist educators* (San Francisco: Jossey-Bass).

Ollman, B. (2003) *Dance of the dialectic: Steps in Marx's method* (Champaign-Urbana: University of Illinois Press).

Rikowski, G. (1996) 'Left alone: End time for Marxist educational theory?', *British Journal of Sociology of Education*, Vol. 17, No. 4, 415–51.

— (1997) 'Scorched earth: Prelude to rebuilding Marxist educational theory', *British Journal of Sociology of Education*, Vol. 18, No. 4, 551–74.

— (2001) 'After the manuscript broke off: thoughts on Marx, social class and education', *Education Study Group*, presentation, British Sociological Association (BSA), London. Retrieved from www.leeds.ac.uk/educol/documents/00001931.htm.

Sayer, D. (1987) *The violence of abstraction: The analytical foundations of historical materialism* (London: Blackwell).

Smith, D. (1990) *The conceptual practices of power: A feminist sociology of knowledge* (Toronto: University of Toronto Press).

— (2011) 'Ideology, science, and social relations: A reinterpretation of Marx's epistemology', in S. Carpenter and S. Mojab (eds), *Educating from Marx: Race, gender, and learning* (New York: Palgrave Macmillan), pp. 19–40.

Thompson, J. (ed.) (1980) *Adult education for a change* (London: Hutchinson).

— (1982) *Radical adult education: Theory and practice* (Nottingham: University of Nottingham).

— (1983) *Learning liberation: Women's response to men's education* (London: Taylor & Francis).

— (1997) *Words in edgeways: Radical learning for social change* (Leicester: NIACE).

Walter, P. (2003) 'Literacy, imagined nations, and imperialism: Frontier College and the construction of British Canada, 1899–1933', *Adult Education Quarterly*, Vol. 54, No. 1, 42–58.

Wangoola, P. and Youngman, F. (eds) (1996) *Towards a transformative political economy of adult education: Theoretical and practical challenges* (DeKalb, IL: LEPS).

Welton, M.R. (1995) *In defense of the lifeworld: Critical perspectives on adult learning* (Sunnybrook: SUNY Press).

— (2001) *Little Mosie from the Margaree: A biography of Moses Michael Coady* (Toronto: Thompson Educational).

Wood, E.M. (1995) *Democracy against capitalism: Renewing historical materialism* (Cambridge: Cambridge University Press).

— (2003) *Empire of capital* (London: Verso).

Youngman, F. (1986) *Adult education and socialist pedagogy* (London: Croom Helm).

— (2000) *The political economy of adult education and development* (London: Zed).

3

Learning and the 'Matter' of Consciousness in Marxist Feminism

In teaching, a major challenge for us is to help students articulate the sources of their knowledge about themselves or the world. We ask them to think through epistemological questions. How do you know what you know? Where does your knowledge come from? There are some immediate and predictable answers such as personal experience, accumulated academic or work related knowledge, or social learning through culture, tradition, media, or personal or group interaction. We encourage them to go deeper in their explanation and interpretation of social relations and their role and location in them. This, we have come to realize, is not an easy process, in part because, in our understanding, the way to answer these questions is to articulate the relationship between self and the social world as well as between consciousness and the material world. Often students are neither able to name this relationship nor are they fully capable of articulating their location in these social relations. Thus, as teachers, we have found it necessary to delve deeper into the problematic of dissociated self and society. In this chapter, we undertake an exploration of the relation between consciousness and the material world from the perspective of Marxist feminism.

The conceptualization of consciousness is a central component of a Marxist theory of education and learning and has grown in recent years through the work of authors such as Paula Allman, Wayne Au, John Holst, Helen Colley, Peter McLaren and Nathalia Jaramillo, and the continued exploration of Freire's and Gramsci's seminal works (Allman, 2007; Au, 2007a; Colley, 2002; Holst, 1999; Mayo, 1999; McLaren and Jaramillo, 2010). The transformation of consciousness is an important aim of critical education's historical legacy of social movement mobilization, popular education and trade-union organizing (Rikowski 1996, 1997). Despite this centrality, the theorization of consciousness largely takes place in other arenas of social theory and, noticeably, almost exclusively by radical scholars from feminist theory, psychoanalytic theory, critical race theory and Marxism. We observe that in critical theories of education consciousness is often treated as an object of pedagogical intervention; the phrases 'critical consciousness', 'consciousness raising' and 'conscientization' are expressed as outcomes, process, methods or goals. The outcome of this practice is to disconnect consciousness from its theoretical roots and, ultimately, to de-radicalize the purpose of talking about consciousness in the first place. Part of this problem may be traced to educators confining their reading on consciousness to Freire, or reading his work in an essentially liberalized or pragmatic vision divorced from its roots in Marxist humanism (Allman and Wallis, 1990; Au, 2007a). As Marxist feminist researchers and educators, we find the theorization of consciousness to be essential not only to our imagination of pedagogical possibilities, but also to understanding the realities of the social relations and conditions we research and try to explain.

We begin this chapter from Paula Allman's argument that Marx's theorization of consciousness is central for critical education theory, as well as for understanding the role of education in the reproduction of labour and capitalist social relations (Allman, 1999, 2001, 2007). For Allman, the Marxist theorization of consciousness is in fact the theorization of praxis. However, we seek to go further into the social relations elucidated in Allman's work by providing a reading of consciousness from a Marxist feminist perspective. To do this, we have organized this discussion in three parts. First, we review Marx's original articulation of his theory of consciousness. This review, which draws heavily from Allman's work as well as that of Derek Sayer (1979; 1987), positions our reading of consciousness dialectically and historically. Second, we provide a historical review of the development of the theorization of consciousness in educational theory in order to give the reader a sense of how this theorization has evolved as part of the ongoing political struggles of Marxism, feminism and anti-racism. Third, we examine feminist-materialist expansions of Marx's theory of consciousness and argue that through these feminist interventions we can see more deeply into Marx's notion of social totality and into the complex and changing organization of capitalist social relations. We conclude by sketching some of the implications of a Marxist feminist perspective for consciousness in the field of adult education.

Consciousness in Marx

Marx's discussion of consciousness began with what, from our vantage point, may appear as an abstract philosophical debate. In the wake of Hegel's death, a group of young, radical philosophers began their academic and activist lives, calling themselves the 'Young Hegelians'. Initially Marx was one of these young men committed to freeing human consciousness from the strangleholds of religious and secular monarchy (Callinicos, 1999). However, he eventually broke from this group over an extremely important question: Who makes history? Or: How is history made? In the Hegelian framework, history is made, determined and advanced through the development of rational human consciousness. This consciousness exists only in the human mind or spirit, and Hegel referred to it as 'absolute'. Hegel's argument was a pure form of idealism, in which the existence of objective reality is only made possible through human consciousness. In this schema, consciousness determines life (Warminski, 1995).

The Young Hegelians exchanged this absolute idealism for what they knew as 'materialism': an inversion of the Hegelian reliance on 'the spirit'. They argued that the relation between the ideal and the material had to be inverted: the material determined the ideal (Arthur, 1991). In this formulation, human consciousness was treated as an effluence; it is the thing that comes after and corresponds to its precursor (Allman, 2001). Beginning in the mid 1840s, Marx and Engels began a series of critiques of Hegel and his successors. This critique developed from *A Contribution to the Critique of Hegel's Philosophy of Right* (1843) to *The Holy Family* (1844), *The German Ideology* (1845–46) and *The Poverty of Philosophy* (1847). In these 'early' texts, Marx and Engels systematically dismantled the arguments of the Young Hegelians. Marx commented on this relation, saying:

> My inquiry led to the conclusion that neither legal relations nor political forms could be comprehended whether by themselves or on the basis of a so-called general development of the human mind, but that on the contrary they originate in the material conditions of life, the totality of which Hegel, following the example of English and French thinkers of the eighteenth century, embraces within the term

'civil society'; that the anatomy of this civil society, however, has to be sought in political economy. (1970, p. 20)

In their critique of philosophical idealism, Marx and Engels conferred on matter a determining role, although in their critique of mechanistic materialism they insisted that the relationship between consciousness and matter could not be understood as one of determination (Marx and Engels, 1968). This relation of determination, however, is extremely complex and forms the central feature of the base-superstructure debate. From a dialectical position, the two enter into relations of unity and struggle of opposites, meaning that the ideal and the material mutually determine one another through an internal relation. To establish this internal relation, Marx and Engels had to refute Hegel's emphasis on the 'absolute' ideal at the same time as refuting the 'absolute' materialism of the Young Hegelians. Establishing this dialectical relation poses a significant challenge to Marxist thinkers.

This dialectic was not seen by the Young Hegelians, such as Feuerbach, for whom reality was only considered as *'the object of contemplation*, but not as *sensuous human activity, practice*, not subjectively' (Marx, 1968, p. 659). The relation between the ideal and the material was essential for Marx because of its implications for human practice. In both the subjective idealism of Hegel and the contemplative materialism of Feuerbach, human agency was subtext rather than the engine of history. History and reality moved around and passed people, as if they were passive observers of a world moving without them. For Marx, history and social reality were sensuous human activity. Thus, in direct opposition to the dogmatic interpretation of Marxism as a science that obliterates the subject, Marx insisted on the power of people to transform the world. For Marx, our consciousness is nothing less than conscious life, meaning that consciousness and matter are locked in a dialectical relation with one another in which they constantly form and transform their essence and appearance through struggle and movement. This dialectical unity of opposites, a major organizing principle of Marx's philosophy and science, is conditioned by a kind of materialism in which the sensuous activity of people *over time* is central to its conception. Marx argued that the social life of people, understood as the ways in which they produce and reproduce themselves materially and socially, was historically specific. Everyone, he argued, must contend with history. We act, we think, we resist, we organize ourselves, but not under conditions of our choosing (Marx, 1979).

Marx's understanding of consciousness is complex and related to another important formulation: social reality. Marx's ontology, which he and Engels put forward in *The German Ideology*, is based not only on historical specificity but also on the notion of human co-operative activity (Marx and Engels, 1968). For Marx and Engels, human life would not exist without humans living and working in co-operative social relations in order to produce and reproduce their lives. These co-operative relations are not necessarily peaceful, but rather co-operative in the sense that humans live and reproduce socially – their existence is evidence of the social nature of life, and language is the most indelible proof of this connection (Marx, 1974; McNally, 2001). However, one of the central characteristics of life within a capitalist mode of production is that we do not experience our lives as social or co-operative. Rather, we work under the conception that we are individual, independent and self-sufficient (see Wilde, 1994, for an interesting elaboration of this point). One of the easiest ways to understand this tension is to take a moment and think about where your food comes from. For some of us, we may be able to say that we grew our food on our own land. The rest of us will acknowledge that our food arrives on our table through a vast network of human relations in which active human labour takes place at every level. This co-operative behaviour demonstrates the social organization of the relations of production. It also demonstrates that we do not experience the world on a daily basis as the subjective reality that reflects these complex relations. When we go to the grocery store, we do not think about all the people whose lives are found in the product that winds up in the cereal aisle. Rather, we just think about the objects of human labour and, frankly, we do not think of other people as part of the same social relations as ourselves. They disappear in the objectification of social life we experience every day. For Marx, this relation of objectivity and subjectivity is inherent to the explanation of the relation between consciousness and matter. Consciousness exists in both subjective and objective forms, as does matter. The objectification takes place on the level of consciousness and in real, everyday life. It is this objectification and its formation in consciousness that Marx and Engels refer to in their famous analogy of the *camera obscura*, in which people 'and their circumstances appear upside-down' (Marx and Engels, 1968, p. 37).

In other terms, the relation between consciousness and matter can be understood as the relation between epistemology and ontology. Ontology, which we have discussed above, refers to the theorization of actually existing reality. For Marx, reality does objectively exist, but it exists dialectically in the co-operative labour of people *and* their forms of consciousness. What is of the utmost importance for the theorization of consciousness is how this reality can be *known*. These are the questions we ask our students in class and with which we began this chapter. How do we know what we know? Where does our knowledge come from? The philosophical articulation of this relation has extremely important implications for the practice of revolutionary struggle. For instance, Mao Tse-Tung's contribution to this debate, in the context of the Chinese Revolution, was to argue that in the realm of ontology it is impossible to differentiate between consciousness and matter (Mao Tse-Tung, 2007). However, on the terrain of epistemology we can come to know 'the mechanism by which thought can have access to and come to know objectively the realm of reality' (Knight, 2005, p. 175). What is established in the ontology–epistemology relation is the philosophy of praxis, which Mao referred to as practice-based epistemology, and which unites consciousness and matter in a dialectical relation in which consciousness can come to know reality *and* move beyond the experiential and situated appearances of matter.

In a way similar to Mao (Knight, 1990) and Gramsci (Thomas, 2009), Paula Allman (2001) has argued that Marx's theory of consciousness cannot be understood as anything other than a philosophy of praxis. Understanding the relation between consciousness and matter within capitalist social life is very tricky, and Allman has done an invaluable service to educators by developing a heuristic tool to help us think about the relation between praxis, human agency and historical change. For Allman, the logical extension of Marx's argument is that human praxis can exist in two very divergent forms. On the one hand, we can live in such a way that reproduces the violence, oppression and exploitation of capitalist life. This form of praxis, which Allman (2007) calls reproductive or uncritical, does not interrogate the roots of social relations. It may be able to describe the effects or consequences of capitalist social relations, but it cannot locate their source and, further, it cannot move beyond the *appearance* of these relations. An alternative is critical or revolutionary praxis. This form of praxis requires seeking out the forms of consciousness that dig below the surface of capitalism's appearances and into its *essences*, the dialectical contradictions that form the relations of everyday life.

Another way to refer to these characteristics is to describe them as terms of engagement with the *phenomenal forms* of capitalism, capitalism's appearance, or rather, its ideologically objectified forms of social consciousness (Sayer, 1987; Bannerji, 2015). These characteristics reproduce the separations and inversions of capitalist social relations that obliterate the visibility of dialectical contradictions in everyday life. Each of these forms of consciousness, or ways of thinking, is part of what 'Marx describes as the "violence of *abstraction*", when one's thinking reproduces the separation of the opposites that constitute a unity of opposites, an internal relation, when it "violently abstracts", it distorts one's understanding' (Allman, 2007, p. 35). Consciousness formed through abstraction, which Marx referred to as 'the imagined concrete', ultimately happens because of the very nature of social life within capitalism. We do not often experience daily life in such a way that the relations between phenomena are seen; in fact, we often experience these relations, such as violence against women and labour exploitation, temporally and in spatially disparate ways, and thus we see their 'appearance' in capitalist social relations although not their 'essence' (Colley, 2002). Thus, it is equally important to remember that these forms of consciousness are not 'errors' in logic as much as they are 'grounded in capitalism's phenomenal forms, the ways in which the social relations of bourgeois society present themselves to the consciousness of its participants' (Sayer, 1987, p. 130).

Many of the concepts Allman describes as characteristics are related to the larger social relation of *alienation* (Allman, 2007). Alienation is not essentially a pathological emotional state, although in its extreme forms it may emerge as such. An excellent example of this process can be found in the memoir *Rivethead: Tales from the Assembly Line*, in which the author painstakingly details the emergence of physical and psychological self-abuse as a response to the violence of factory life (Hamper, 1992). Alienation is in fact a social process and relation in which individuals are divorced from their humanist vocation, the 'process of becoming' in Marx's terms, by giving up or surrendering their power and potential to an external force (either a person or a thing) that in turn uses that power against the individual. Once given away, human power appears to us as something outside ourselves, and alienation becomes manifested in the appearance of opposition between individuals and things, rather than a struggle within the relations of capitalism.

Alienation is often manifested in *dichotomized thought*. Dichotomies, so often the target of critical analysis, are pervasive in reproductive praxis because they obliterate the existence of relations – particularly inner relations – and complexity in social life. In a dichotomy, something cannot be logically understood as two things at the same time, as opposed to a dialectical relation in which a phenomenon is composed of mutually determining components locked in struggle. Dichotomies are an expression of the ongoing experiential separation of contradictory social relations. A second process that contributes to this experiential separation is the tendency towards *reification* in bourgeois thought. Reification is simply taking social processes and relations and making them into 'things'. We sometimes find it helpful to remind ourselves that the verb to reify is akin to petrify; both take something alive and transform its movement into stasis and lifelessness. In a particularly grotesque about-face, an extreme characteristic of reification is personification. A classic example is Marx's analysis of money, which he argues is essentially a commodity expressing a number of complex human relations. Within the historical development of capitalist relations, money becomes a thing that can be hoarded. It even becomes a person, given agency and power in society. As such, 'money talks'. In its most developed form, reification becomes 'a form of distortion where the attributes and powers, the essence, of the person or the social relation appear as natural, intrinsic, attributes or powers of the "thing"' (Allman, 2007, p. 37). This is *fetishism*, 'the ultimate objective and subjective expression of alienation in human practice' (p. 37). In capitalist society, we believe that the value of money is intrinsic to its material form. We see money as an end in itself rather than symbolic of the labour of billions of people reduced to the exchange of commodities mediated by the universal commodity, money. Allman argues that fetishism is the dialectical relation of alienation. As we produce within capitalism we negate ourselves through the labour–capital relation; as we consume we also negate ourselves and everyone else.

As we can see, the dialectical formation of consciousness and matter is rife with complexity. The ultimate outcomes of bourgeois thought are to make this complexity invisible in order to naturalize and normalize capitalist social relations. A simple way to do this is through *conflation*, which 'involves a futile attempt to eliminate complexity by taking entities that are separated and reuniting them by equating them, or in philosophical terms, establishing an immediate identity between them' (Allman, 2007, p. 38). Conflation is easily seen in the bourgeois claim of the trans-historical nature of market-based social relations. 'To Marx, conflated thinking was both simplistic and distorted, particularly because it encouraged people to ignore historically specific differences as well as the essential internal relations, i.e. the internally specific (but not identical) nature of various entities and processes' (p. 38). By eliminating history and contradiction, conflation, in concert with other forms of reproductive praxis, performs a second level of violent abstraction. Not only is the unity of dialectical relations ruptured, but the social relations of material life are broken up into composite parts. Relations such as gender, race, sexuality and class are divorced from one another and appear as autonomous. The feminist theorizing of intersectionality, interlocking oppression, or matrices of domination demonstrates the role of conflation in consciousness; having artificially separated these social relations they are reunited in a 'mystical' way (Aguilar, 2010; 2015). These two kinds of abstraction, the separation of life and relations and their reunification through unknown processes, constitute the core of the method of ideological knowledge production (Bannerji, 2011; 2015), discussed in more detail in Chapter 5. However, while all consciousness requires some kind of abstraction, not all abstractions must be ideological. Marx and Engels argued that through the method of dialectical historical materialism, abstraction could be used in order to fully explicate the essence of dialectically contradictory relations. It is this form of consciousness, as we will show below, which has become the epistemological imperative of the Marxist theorization of education and learning.

The roots of critical consciousness

Our purpose in this section is to historicize, albeit briefly, a component of the theoretical underpinnings of the approaches to consciousness used in critical education. We recognize that it would be a separate undertaking to expand this section to include the full range of authors on this subject, thus we have limited this discussion to those who have been most significant to educators and who have attempted to follow Marx's method of dialectical conceptualization, including Lenin, Vygotsky, Gramsci, Lukács, Mao and Freire. It is important that radical educators be familiar with this historical trajectory in order to guard against a tendency in social science to disconnect theoretical categories from their full social development, a tendency implicated in the larger project of ideological knowledge production (Smith, 1990). We draw on the contributions of feminist theory, particularly Dorothy E. Smith's work on consciousness, in the latter part of this chapter. We have observed that there are three important threads running through this body of knowledge: the relation between consciousness and matter; the everyday versus the scientific; and the processes of abstraction and generalization.

After Marx the theorization of consciousness became deeply embroiled with the question of revolution. While this connection, that is, the problem of how to transform human consciousness for the purposes of revolution, may appear obvious on the surface, the debates about this relation have been deep and far reaching. A major turning point in this debate was set by Lenin in his 1902 pamphlet *What is to be Done?* Lenin's discussion provides an excellent starting point for tracing the nuances in the theorization of consciousness as he sets out the central problematic of the debate. *What is to be Done?* was a response to the ongoing debate in the late nineteenth and early twentieth centuries about the strategic development of revolution in Russia, particularly the role of consciousness in the transformation of organized action. Lenin focused his discussion on the theorization of the proletariat's responses to the abuses of capital. He differentiated between what he sees as spontaneous forms of consciousness, which take the form of strikes, revolts, riots or uprisings, and conscious action, which takes the form of organized working-class struggle. He argued:

> Taken by themselves, these strikes were simply trade union struggles, not yet social-democratic struggles. They marked the awakening antagonism between workers and employers; but the workers were not, and could not be, conscious of the irreconcilable antagonism of their interests to the whole of the modern political and social system, i.e. theirs was not yet social-democratic consciousness. (1978, p. 31)

Lenin argues that while the conditions of work had spurred the workers on to rebellion, the consciousness driving their activity was not formulated in terms of the dialectical relations of labour–capital nor in a particularly historical way. His central challenge is to argue that this form of consciousness is imperative in order for socialist mobilization to move beyond reformist programmes. In this way, Lenin identified dialectical and historical analysis as components of what we might call 'critical consciousness'.

Lenin and Marx both argued that revolutionary change – that is, the replacement of an obsolete social formation by a new, progressive one – was a conscious act rather than a spontaneous development. Although individuals act consciously rather than instinctually and societies do change spontaneously, the creation of a new social formation such as classless society cannot be accomplished without knowledge, and especially revolutionary theory, leadership and organization. While this is evident in the work of Marx and Engels, it was Lenin who, in *What is to be Done?*, addressed the questions involved in the revolutionary transition from capitalism to socialism led by social-democratic parties in Russia and the rest of Europe. Lenin argued that the economic struggle of workers does not provide an adequate basis for the political consciousness necessary to overthrow the capitalist system because such consciousness requires knowledge about all social classes, their contradictions and expectations, and their relation to government and the state. Such political consciousness can come '*only from without*, that is, only from outside the economic struggle, from outside the sphere of relations between workers and employers. The sphere from which alone it is possible to obtain this knowledge is the sphere of relationship of *all classes*' (1978, p. 78). Socialist consciousness requires, according to Lenin, knowledge of theory as well as sciences which should be brought into the working-class movement by socialists. Many critics of Lenin have accused him of 'elitism' and anti-worker bias for distinguishing between social-democratic consciousness and trade-union consciousness, and arguing that the 'trade-unionist politics of the working class is precisely *bourgeois politics* of the working class...' (p. 83, emphasis in the original; for a survey of the critics and critique of *What is to be Done?*, see Shandro 1995).

Lenin's claims about the distinction between the two types of consciousness and two movements, working-class and social-democratic (communist), is, far from betraying elitist bias, based on his dialectical understanding of capitalism, and the network of contradictions such as that between manual and mental labour, matter and consciousness, spontaneity and consciousness, theory and practice, and essence and appearance. From Lenin's perspective, capitalism could not transform into socialism spontaneously as capitalism had developed from feudalism. Thus, in the transition to socialism, consciousness determines matter; this explains why Lenin insisted, as Engels had done, that 'without revolutionary theory there can be no revolutionary movement' (1978, p. 25). Trade-union activism, which advocates better wages, adequate living conditions, and favourable legislation, is a just struggle of the workers; its bourgeois nature is, according to Lenin, the politics of not seeking the replacement of the capitalist system by socialism. Lenin's insistence that the 'economic struggle' of the workers and 'the sphere of relations between workers and employers' do not provide adequate bases for understanding the revolutionary transformation of capitalism means that theoretical struggle requires knowledge of history and sciences. This is what has been denied to workers, due, among other things, to the historical divide between mental and manual labour. Lenin emphasized that revolutionary change needed '*professional revolutionaries*, irrespective of whether they have developed from among students or working men' (p. 121.)

Although a long-debated issue, we here follow Harding (1996), who argued that the premises of Lenin's discussion are taken from Marx. Harding contended that Lenin understood consciousness and matter, as philosophical concepts, to be in a dialectical relation, meaning that the two stand in unity and struggle. For Lenin, matter includes everything outside of our bodies, including the consciousness of other human beings. In this way, the relation of consciousness and matter is also the relation of the individual to the social whole. Lenin's problem, and that of the communist movement, is that while the consciousness of workers is based on observing and experiencing labour conditions, daily experience does not necessarily lead to a theoretical understanding of those conditions themselves. Lenin pointed out, as many of us may have recognized ourselves, that most workers will not arrive, through their own experience, at the same conclusions to which Engels and Marx arrived on their own. However, Lenin observed an important contradiction. Engels did not begin his intellectual life as a socialist or communist;

he was a factory owner and, like many other members of his class, was expected to justify the exploitation of the working class. That he was able to change sides and advocate the interests of workers was primarily because of his study of theory and history and due to a political decision to change the world. Lenin employed a dialectical understanding of the relation between consciousness and matter, one in which human agents are not psychically or intellectually trapped in the conditions in which they find themselves. This dialectical relationship has been expressed in different ways in Marxist literature, including in Mao Tse-Tung's statement that 'matter can be transformed into consciousness and consciousness into matter' (2007, p. 136).

Lenin formulated his terminology through the concepts of the spontaneous and the conscious. The spontaneous, for Lenin, refers to the consciousness of life formed through everyday experiences. Spontaneous consciousness must exist as, given Marx's dialectical formulation, life cannot be anything other than conscious life. Spontaneous consciousness, so often cast in a pejorative light, is of the utmost importance to Lenin. Spontaneity, however, is understood as somehow different from conscious activity. It is important to recognize that Lenin and Marx use the terms consciousness and conscious in different ways. Marx is entering the German Idealist debate about the relationships between matter and consciousness. He is demonstrating how consciousness is dialectically related to the social organization of life and exists in both objective and subjective forms. Lenin is talking about consciousness in relation to the formation of a political agenda necessary to revolution. Thus, to be 'conscious' is to have the kind of consciousness that relates to revolutionary practice. Lenin is moving into the theorization of how to organize thinking and ideas in a revolutionary manner based on the dialectical theorization of Marx.

Of particular importance to educators are the similarities between Lenin's framework and Lev Vygotsky's educational theory. There is much debate concerning the role of Marxism in Vygotsky's work. What is unavoidable, and persuasively argued by Wayne Au (2007b), is that there is a definite historical and theoretical linkage between the two, which, taken together, constitute an important dimension of our contemporary thinking on the question of consciousness. Au has argued that Vygotsky uses the terms 'everyday' and 'scientific' to mirror Lenin's differentiation of the spontaneous and the conscious. In Vygotsky's paradigm, 'everyday concepts' refer to Marx's original assertion that we are always conscious persons who move through the world, think, act, make decisions and choices, learn, and so on. Scientific concepts, however, are qualitatively different in that they do not relate to a conscious awareness of reality as immediately given but to 'an act of consciousness whose object is the activity of consciousness itself' (Vygotsky in Au, 2007b, p. 280). To be conscious is 'to be actively conscious of your consciousness in a systemic way' (p. 280). Au argues that Vygotsky understood these concepts (of the scientific and everyday) to be dialectically related, or a 'unified process of concept formation' (p. 282). In this dialectical formulation Vygotsky found psychology to be inseparable from sociology, meaning that individual consciousness, the psyche, could not be understood apart from social relations and social forms of consciousness (Jones, 2009).

While Vygotsky is often reduced in learning theory to discussions of zones, scaffolds and activity, he continues in the Marxist tradition of theorizing praxis. Marx's original theory of praxis, which is unfolded in his discussion of consciousness, is dependent on his empirical demonstration that 'the principle of change in our social world was based on the movement and development of dialectical contradictions' (Allman and Wallis, 1990, p. 14). Embodied in the notion of praxis we find the theorization of consciousness as well as the dialectical formation of the relation between spontaneous or everyday forms of consciousness and scientific or conscious consciousness. Arguably one of the most sophisticated formulations of praxis in the Marxist tradition is that of Mao Tse-Tung (2007). Again, Mao rejects all dualism on the plane of ontology, meaning that for him consciousness is matter as well, a particular social product of the characteristics of the human mind, while epistemology requires a forced dualism so that humans may be able to understand their own processes of consciousness, or how they come to know the contours of their material life (Knight, 1990). To put it another way: in everyday life, consciousness and matter struggle with one another in a dialectical relation. We move, both consciously and unconsciously, through the world, constantly mediating experience with meaning. However, in order to understand and make sense of daily life, to reflect on what we know and how we know it, we must conceptualize our consciousness independently of its intimate relation to material reality, even as it is constantly formed in this relation. This is a meta-theoretical position; while we all exist in the realm of 'spontaneous' consciousness, we can also understand ourselves in such a sophisticated way that we can operate above the level of everyday understandings and appearances. This is the formation of the two kinds of praxis to which Allman refers (1999, 2001, 2007).

Because of this dialectical formulation, scientific consciousness must emerge in relation to spontaneous forms. Lenin argued that spontaneous, rebellious activity was the ground from which a revolutionary consciousness would emerge (Holst, 1999). The emergence of such a transformation, however, was premised on the role of hegemony and the pedagogical activities of political parties. These conditions give rise to ongoing debates concerning the role of hegemony, so-called 'organic intellectuals', vanguards, and the power relations implied therein. Our purposes here require that we focus on the dialectical formulation behind these questions: the implication that learning to think differently about life requires the recognition of spontaneous consciousness as consciousness. This is not the same thing as the pragmatic preference for all things experiential, in which all knowledge that emerges from experience is treated as differing shades of truth. Rather, experience is not fetishized but becomes the object of reality that can be understood through the application of concepts. This is the approach to experience taken by Marx throughout his work. Imagine Marx in nineteenth-century London, living in a part of the city, present-day Soho, that had been notorious for its poverty, deprivation, filth, disease, crime and pestilence for several hundred years; conditions so horrible that the community was blamed for the onset of the plague (Ackroyd, 2009). Somehow Marx goes from the everyday experience of this crisis to his scientific understanding of capitalism, just as Engels goes from the tedium of organizing a factory to a revolutionary communist position. This is the process we are trying to understand.

An important component of Lenin's argument is that the movement from the spontaneous to the conscious, the transformation of consciousness, happens through learning to think abstractly about concrete social conditions and relations. Lenin argued that processes of abstraction and generalization, based in historical materialist analysis and not idealism, are necessary in order for workers to see past the immediate struggle for rights, wages and conditions (the 'economist' argument) and into the totality of a social whole premised on violence and exploitation (Lenin, 1978). The ways in which we understand the categories of abstraction and generalization are extremely important in the divergences of the theorization of consciousness in the Marxist tradition. For example, Derek Sayer has devoted much attention to uncovering the ways in which these categories are misunderstood in structuralist Marxism and which result in the mechanistic separation of the ideal and the material, which reproduces the forms of abstraction Marx and Engels described in their critique of the Young Hegelians (Sayer, 1987). Lenin envisioned the role of abstraction as both theoretical and pedagogical, arguing that 'it is possible to "begin" only by inducing people to think about all these things, by inducing them to summarize and generalize all of the diverse signs of ferment and active struggle' (1978, p. 231). This method of abstraction, generalization and summation, however, had to be based in a dialectical understanding of history.

Au argues that Vygotsky built on this theorization of the emergence of consciousness through abstraction and generalization. For Vygotsky, consciousness was 'conscious awareness', which he explained in this way:

> If conscious awareness means generalization, it is obvious that gener-
> alization, in turn, means nothing other than the formation of a higher
> concept in a system of generalization that includes the given concept
> as a particular case ... Thus, the generalization of the concept leads to
> its localization within a definite system of relationships of generality
> ... Thus at one and the same time, generalization implies the conscious
> awareness and the systematization of concepts. (Vygotsky cited by Au,
> 2007b, p. 279)

Both Lenin and Vygotsky were working with a relationship between higher order theoretical conceptualization and a conscious mastery of a complex system of relations. Critical educators will recognize in this formulation the roots of Freire's generative themes and the process of moving from everyday experience to a larger meta-thematic organization of systemic relations (Freire, 1971). Freire describes the process as movement from the general to the particular and back out to the general. He argues: 'When people lack a critical understanding of their reality, apprehending it in fragments which they do not perceive as interacting constituent elements of the whole, they cannot truly know the reality' (1971, p. 85).

The purpose of the theorization of consciousness, as Marx (1968) famously declares in the 'Theses on Feuerbach', is not only to understand the world, but to change it. However, Freire's argument that we cannot truly know our reality when we apprehend it in fragments is a critique that echoes across the Marxist and neo-Marxist theorizations of consciousness. Marxists are not the only critical scholars who have taken up this question; feminist and anti-racist scholars have also devoted considerable time to constructing a body of knowledge around the question of consciousness. Their work illuminates a component of consciousness that is difficult, but not impossible, to see from the Marxist perspective.

Expanding praxis through Marxist feminist analysis

We have observed that there is a difference between the Marxist theorization of consciousness and the discussions of consciousness that circulate amongst feminist and critical race theorists. It is our hope to bring these conversations closer together. The most salient divergence is the emphasis in feminist and critical race theory on a felt duality in the consciousness of women and people of colour in capitalist life. This duality has been described as 'bifurcated', 'outsider-within', and, famously, as 'double consciousness' (Collins, 2000; Du Bois, 1897, 1987). Du Bois provided a visceral sense of this duality, formed through conflict and struggle, when he said:

> It is a peculiar sensation, this double-consciousness, this sense of always looking at one's self through the eyes of others, of measuring one's soul by the tape of a world that looks on in amused contempt and pity. One ever feels his twoness, – an American, a Negro; two souls, two thoughts, two unreconciled strivings; two warring ideals in one dark body, whose dogged strength alone keeps it from being torn asunder. (1987, p. 3)

We want to argue that these alternative theorizations offer important insights to Marxist scholars that have been sidestepped in the historical development of the body of knowledge around consciousness (Guy and Brookfield, 2009). Here we will primarily discuss feminist theory, but similar themes have been developed through a wide variety of anti-racist and anti-colonial scholarship (Bakan and Dua, 2014; Bakan, 2008; Chibber, 2013; Fanon, 2008; Sekyi-Otu, 1996).

The theorization of consciousness was a core component of feminist movements throughout the twentieth century. Consciousness-raising groups proliferated, particularly during the 1960s and 1970s, in response to the growing awareness by women of the systematic and widespread nature of gendered and sexualized oppression. Research on feminist consciousness expanded throughout the 1980s and seemed to find a home in cultural and psychological explanations of the phenomenon. The phenomenon under interrogation was how it is that women come to see themselves not just as individual women in interpersonal relations of domination or violence, but understand these social conditions as a universal gender relation of patriarchy. Mojab has described this differentiation as 'feminine' versus 'feminist' consciousness, and it expresses a deep similarity to Lenin's articulation of spontaneous and scientific forms of consciousness and Vygotsky's emphasis on the movement from the individual to the social (Mojab, 2001). It is important to acknowledge that both academic and political work on feminist consciousness has largely focused on describing the psychosocial and emotional components of gendered oppression. To the extent that these experiences are explained in feminist theory, their derivation is largely attributed to the realm of culture. This focus on culture may provide a historical linkage to the experience of exploitation or deprivation, but the arena of feminist politics is confined to language, ideas, representation or discursive transformation. This orientation can be seen in a theoretical resistance amongst feminists to the concept of patriarchy, ironically in sharp contrast to the acknowledgement of patriarchy as the historical impetus for feminist consciousness raising and its social movement orientations (Bannerji, 2016; Mojab, 2010; Sangari, 2015).

Dorothy E. Smith contends that the inclination to see women's experience as primarily cultural performs the dangerous processes of abstraction described by Marx (Smith, 1988). Smith argues that the focus must move from culture to ideology. Moving from culture to ideology 'directs us to examine who produces what for whom, where the social forms of consciousness come from' (1988, p. 54). Smith's argument is beyond ideology critique. Rather, she argues that a feminist theorization of experience and consciousness (or praxis) must begin with the *social* forms of consciousness. In other words, understanding consciousness in both subjective and objective forms directs our attention away from the *effects* of gendered oppression and towards the analysis of patriarchy as a universalizing social relation (Ebert, 1996).

One of the contributions of Marxist feminist theory is its ability to marshal the subjective experience of patriarchy as a way of seeing into larger social relations in order to understand where and how both subjective and objective forms of consciousness arise. This conversation is complicated by the implications of feminist epistemology. Feminists of many different theoretical orientations have toyed with the notion of epistemic privilege, or the idea that women, by virtue of their social location within racist, patriarchal, capitalist social relations, produce a form of knowledge that can only be generated from a particular subject position (Anzaldúa, 1987; Alcoff and Potter, 1993; Collins, 2000; Haraway, 1988; Harding, 2004). This assertion has been the cause of a tremendous amount of debate amongst feminists and its core epistemo-logical assertion has constituted at least one reading of Lukács (Jameson, 1988). As Marxist feminists we reject the argument for epistemic privilege that insists there is something exclusively experiential about the ability to understand the realities of racism and sexism, particularly for the purposes of transforming these social relations. Instead, we gravitate towards Dorothy E. Smith's notion of standpoint, itself a hotly contested theoretical topic in feminism with various iterations circulating in the literature (Cockburn, 2015).

Feminist standpoint theory emerged in the 1970s as a response to the exclusion of women's experience from sociological theory and sparked a debate that has raged for more than 30 years (Harding, 2004; Hartsock, 1998; Howard and Allen, 1997). While there have been several permutations of standpoint theory, we work from the ideas articulated by Smith in her critique of sociology and her development of institu-tional ethnography. Smith's perspective on standpoint theory emerged from an understanding of women's labour within the social relations of capitalism. Smith repeats Marx in her understanding that capitalist social relations produce the experiential separation of consciousness and matter. She argues that in modern capitalism this separation is spatially displaced, meaning that:

Capitalism creates a wholly new terrain of social relations external to the local terrain and the particularities of personally mediated economic and social relations. It creates an extra-local medium of action constituted by a market process in which a multiplicity of anonymous buyers and sellers interrelate and by an expanding arena of political activity. These extra-local, impersonal, universalized forms of action became the exclusive terrain of men, while women became correspondingly confined to a reduced local sphere of action organized by particularistic relationships. (1988, p. 5)

For Smith, both the productive and the reproductive labour of women take place within social relations that are not organized on a local, individualized basis. Rather, these relations emerge from a much larger, extra-local social practice. The forms of consciousness dialectically related to these relations similarly emerge from somewhere outside the daily experience of women, which Smith identifies as the objectification of forms of consciousness through the capitalist division of labour. These forms of consciousness can only be produced through the epistemological method of ideology, the violent abstraction of consciousness and matter as well as social and material life (Smith, 2004). As such, what emerges in the daily experience of women is a felt, perceived, immediate dissonance between subjective and objective forms of consciousness.

Smith borrows from Hegel's master–slave parable to provide an example of this formulation. In this parable, Hegel demonstrates that the master and the slave see very different aspects of the world they live in. The master does not worry about how his bed gets made or his food is cooked, nor does he understand the nuances of these processes. The slave, however, has an entirely different perspective on these activities. As Smith notes, 'there is a difference between forms of consciousness arising in the experience of ruling and those arising in the experience of doing the work that creates the conditions of ruling' (1988, p. 80). This parable has often been used as evidence for the claim to epistemic privilege that we have already rejected (Mann and Kelley, 1997). However, another conclusion to draw lies in the argument made by Marx and reviewed by Lukács that there is something in the experience of the proletariat that produces the 'conditions of possibility' for seeing deeply into the organization of social relations and the potential to differentiate between uncritical and critical forms of praxis (Lukács, 1971). Similarly, this qualitative separation provides the basis for a spontaneous consciousness that can be transformed into a scientific consciousness. Without a dialectical understanding of the philosophy of praxis, this notion of 'conditions of possibility', based solely in experience, is impossible.

For Smith, the conditions of possibility are found in the assumption of a feminist standpoint. A feminist standpoint is not epistemic privilege. It is not the idea that only women can know patriarchy or only people of colour can understand racism as relations of power, nor is it the argument that because of a particular subject position one already 'naturally' possesses a scientific, conceptual understanding of oppression. Rather, it is the idea that knowledge production is a political project in which scholars take up a position in relation to objectified forms of consciousness, or rather, ideology. Standpoint is a political, ethical and intellectual commitment to understanding social relations from a materialist vantage point that undoes the violent abstraction of bourgeois thought. At the same time, it is not an argument for the essential nature of the experience of patriarchy, but a claim to the universalism of patriarchy as an organizing practice of social life. As Smith argues:

> When we take up the standpoint of women, we take up a standpoint outside this frame (as an organization of social consciousness). To begin from such a standpoint does not imply a common viewpoint among women. What we have in common is the organization of social relations that has accomplished our exclusion. (1988, p. 78)

Feminist standpoint theory returns us to the dialectical relation of ontology and epistemology and provides a way of grounding and explicating this relation. The contribution of Marxist feminism to the theorization of this relation is to further complicate our dialectical understanding of not only this relation (praxis), but of the constituent components of praxis (consciousness and matter). Standpoint theory is a commitment to work from gendered experiences in the world and argues that feminism is a scientific form of consciousness in which the material world is entered through the actual realities of a social world organized by social relations of gender and race.

The result of working from a feminist standpoint is a significant alteration to the traditional Marxist conception of materiality. We say 'traditional' because from our perspective Marx and Engels' original dialectical formulations of materiality do not *theoretically* exclude the lives of women. For example, Marx and Engels' made reference to the sexual division of labour as the first division of labour, based in slavery and reformed in capitalist life. They both failed, however, to realize this insight in their treatment of reproductive labour. Nevertheless, we take seriously Mao's assertion that materiality includes everything in the world, including consciousness. When this expansive notion of materiality is used, far beyond the reductionist emphasis on 'labour' understood as purposeful and conscious human intervention in nature, or 'production', then scholarship of striking importance emerges. For example, we now know that the experiences of women during 'primitive accumulation' in Europe provide us with an important understanding of capitalism as a way of organizing social life that is entirely dependent on the formulation of some forms of labour as 'value-less' and which is deeply reliant on the hyper-exploitation of women to accomplish its aims (Federici, 2004).

Federici's work is just one example of a growing body of Marxist feminist literature that re-theorizes material life as necessarily gendered and raced, doing away with any notions of abstract materiality. Marxist theorization without a feminist and anti-racist consciousness performs the same violent abstraction it accuses ideologists of performing. While in ideology consciousness is abstracted from materiality, in Marxism without feminism, material life is theorized as abstracted from the social relations that constitute its very essence. For example, Bannerji has analysed race and gender as 'connative clusters of social relations' (2015, p. 110) which are concretized through the dialectical relation of objectified forms of consciousness and material acts. In her formulation, race and gender cannot be understood as cultural formations or discourses or subtexts of class; rather, they exist as the very social relations through which material life is organized under capitalism and through which capitalism developed. This kind of analysis makes a feminist consciousness as necessary as class consciousness. In a theory premised on a dialectical movement between the abstract and the concrete, the violence of abstraction is easily reproduced when the gendered and racialized organization of the social relations of production is ignored. For example, a Marxist analysis of ideology, consciousness and capitalist social relations will help us to understand the necessity of negating the labour–capital contradiction. However, only an anti-racist Marxist feminist analysis will allow us to understand the internal contradictions in the organization of labour and capital themselves. Only in this way can we see that a negation of labour–capital will not necessarily negate the relations of patriarchy or racism. If we return to the notion that consciousness must be theorized on the terrain of an ontology based in dialectical contradictions, then we must realize that a feminist analysis forces us to confront the real, experiential complexity of those dialectical contradictions. Not only does feminist analysis animate the reality of those contradictions, it elucidates a complexity that otherwise cannot be seen and remains in the realm of abstraction.

To conclude: implications for a Marxist feminist pedagogy of consciousness

Having discussed aspects of theoretical and philosophical thinking about consciousness, we will conclude with reflections on the pedagogical and political implications of a Marxist feminist theory of consciousness. The goal of Marxism is to end the misery of human beings through a transition from the present, which Marx called prehistory, to history, that is, a future without classes, and surely without divisions based on gender, race and other social cleavages. If this future ever materializes, it will happen through a conscious negation of the present and the construction of the envisioned future. This consciousness is multifaceted, with Marxist feminist understanding at its very foundation. Marxist feminist consciousness is decisive because capitalism and all social formations reproduce themselves in innumerable ways and individuals cannot, in the absence of a politicized analysis, comprehend and replace a social formation.

In a similar vein, the central goal of feminism is to overcome the misery of patriarchal gender relations, and it has likewise no option but to negate patriarchy and build an alternative to it. This, too, cannot be achieved without Marxist feminist consciousness. And at the same time, patriarchy is an integral part of a socioeconomic formation. In our historical moment, capitalism without patriarchy or patriarchy without capitalism is impossible, and together they constitute a social whole. Hence, feminism and Marxism cannot fall apart.

Hopefully what has become apparent throughout this discussion is that the theorization of consciousness for critical and radical educators cannot rest on notions of 'counter-hegemony' or 'oppositional knowledge'. It is not only the content of knowledge that is important, but the methods we use to generate this understanding and access our social reality. The core of the pedagogy becomes asking students to think about not only *what* they think, but *how* they think. In this sense, the pedagogy we choose is a question of politics: do we promote a consciousness aimed at creating a new world or do we train citizens skilled in reproducing the status quo? Students have not chosen the world in which they are born. Do we push them to create the consciousness and practice that can make and unmake their own history? The answer, for any educator, is primarily political.

References

Ackroyd, P. (2009) *London: A biography* (London: Knopf Doubleday).

Aguilar, D. (2010) 'From triple jeopardy to intersectionality: The feminist perplex', *Comparative Studies of South Asia, Africa, and the Middle East*, Vol. 32, No. 2, 415–28.

— (2015) 'Intersectionality', in S. Mojab (ed.), *Marxism and feminism* (London: Zed), pp. 203–20.

Alcoff, L. and Potter, E. (eds) (1993) *Feminist epistemologies* (New York: Routledge).

Allman, P. (1999) *Revolutionary social transformation: Democratic hopes, political possibilities and critical education* (Westport, CT: Bergin & Garvey).

— (2001) *Critical education against global capitalism: Karl Marx and revolutionary critical education* (Westport, CT: Bergin & Garvey).

— (2007) *On Marx: An introduction to the revolutionary intellect of Karl Marx* (Rotterdam: Sense).

Allman, P. and Wallis, J. (1990) 'Praxis: Implications for "really" radical education', *Studies in the Education of Adults*, Vol. 22, No. 1, 14–30.

Allman, P. and Wallis, J. (1997) 'Commentary: Paulo Freire and the future of the radical tradition', *Studies in the Education of Adults*, Vol. 29, No. 2, 113–20.

Anzaldúa, G. (1987) *Borderlands: The new Mestiza* (San Francisco: Spinsters/ Aunt Lute).

Arthur, C.J. (1991) 'Editor's Introduction', in C.J Arthur (ed.), *The German ideology* (New York: International), pp. 4–34.

Au, W. (2007a) 'Epistemology of the oppressed: The dialectics of Paulo Freire's theory of knowledge', *Journal for Critical Education Policy Studies*, Vol. 5, No. 2. Available at http://www.jceps.com/archives/551.

— (2007b) 'Vygotsky and Lenin on learning: The parallel structures of individual and social development', *Science & Society*, Vol. 71, No. 3, 273–98.

Bakan, A. (2008) 'Marxism and antiracism: Rethinking the politics of difference', *Rethinking Marxism: A Journal of Economics, Culture & Society*, Vol. 20, No. 2, 238–56.

Bakan, A. and Dua, E. (2014) *Theorizing anti-racism: Linkages in Marxism and critical race theories* (Toronto: University of Toronto Press).

Bannerji, H. (2011) *Demography and democracy: Essays on nationalism, gender and ideology* (Toronto: Canadian Scholars' Press).

— (2015) 'Building from Marx: Reflections on "race", gender and class', in S. Mojab (ed.), *Marxism and Feminism* (London: Zed), pp. 102–21.

— (2016) 'Politics and ideology', *Socialist Studies*, Vol. 11, No. 1, 3–22.

Callinicos, A. (1999) *Social theory: A historical introduction* (New York: NYU Press).

Chibber, V. (2013) *Postcolonial theory and the spectre of capital* (London: Verso).

Cockburn, C. (2015) 'Standpoint theory', in S. Mojab (ed.), *Marxism and Feminism* (London: Zed), pp. 331–46.

Collins, P.H. (2000) *Black feminist thought* (2nd edn) (New York: Routledge).

Colley, H. (2002) 'A rough guide to the history of mentoring from a Marxist Feminist Perspective', *Journal of Education for Teaching*, Vol. 28, No. 3, 257–73.

Du Bois, W.E.B. (1897) 'The strivings of the Negro people', *Atlantic Monthly*, August.

— (1987 [1903]) *The souls of Black folk* (New York: Bantam Classics).

Ebert, T.L. (1996) *Ludic feminism and after: Postmodernism, desire, and labor in late capitalism* (Ann Arbor: University of Michigan Press).

Ebert, T.L. and Zavarzadeh, M. (2007) *Class in culture* (New York: Paradigm).

Fanon, F. (2008 [1952]) *Black skin, white masks*, trans. R. Philcox (New York: Grove).

Federici, S. (2004) *Caliban and the witch: Women, the body, and primitive accumulation* (New York: Autonomedia).

Freire, P. (1971) *Pedagogy of the oppressed* (New York: Seabury).

Gilroy, P. (1995) *The Black Atlantic: Modernity and double consciousness* (Cambridge, MA: Harvard University Press).

Guy, T.C. and Brookfield, S. (2009) 'W.E.B. Du Bois' basic American Negro Creed and the associates in Negro folk education: A case of repressive tolerance in the censorship of radical black discourse on adult education', *Adult Education Quarterly*, Vol. 60, No. 1, 65–76.

Hamper, B. (1992) *Rivethead: Tales from the assembly line* (New York: Warner).

Haraway, D. (1988) 'Situated knowledges: The science question in feminism and the privilege of partial perspectives', *Feminist Studies*, Vol. 14, No. 3, 575–99.

Harding, N. (1996) *Leninism* (Durham, NC: Duke University Press).

Harding, S.G. (ed.) (2004) *The feminist standpoint theory reader: Intellectual and political controversies* (New York: Routledge).

Hartsock, N.C.M. (1998) *The feminist standpoint revisited and other essays* (Boulder: Westview).

Holst, J.D. (1999) 'The affinities of Lenin and Gramsci: Implications for radical adult education theory and practice', *International Journal of Lifelong Education*, Vol. 18, No. 5, 407–21.

Howard, J.A. and Allen, C. (eds) (1997) Special Issue: Standpoint Theory, *Signs*, Vol. 22, No. 2.

Jameson, F. (1988) '"History and Class Consciousness" as an "unfinished project"', *Rethinking Marxism*, Vol. 1, No. 1, 49–72.

Jones, P. (2009) 'Breaking away from capital? Theorising activity in the shadow of Marx', *Outlines*, Vol. 1, 45–58.

Knight, N. (ed.) (1990) *Mao Zedong on dialectical materialism: Writing on philosophy, 1937* (London: M.E. Sharpe).

Knight, N. (2005) *Marxist philosophy in China: From Qu Qiubai to Mao Zedong, 1923–1945* (Amsterdam: Springer).

Lenin, V. (1978 [1902]) *What is to be done? Burning questions of our movement* (Moscow: Progress).

Lukács, G. (1971) *History and class consciousness: Studies in Marxist dialectics*, trans. R. Livingstone (Cambridge, MA: MIT Press).

McLaren, P. and Jaramillo, N. (2010) 'Not neo-Marxist, not post-Marxist, not Marxian, not Autonomist Marxism: Reflections on a revolutionary (Marxist) critical pedagogy', *Cultural Studies* ↔ *Critical Methodologies*, Vol. 10, No. 3, 251–62.

McNally, D. (2001) *Bodies of meaning: Studies on language, labor, and liberation* (Albany: SUNY Press).

Mann, S.A. and Kelley, L.R. (1997) 'Standing at the crossroads of modernist thought: Collins, Smith, and the new feminist epistemologies', *Gender and Society*, Vol. 11, No. 4, 391–408.

Mao Tse-Tung (2007) 'On practice and contradiction', in S. Žižek (ed.), *On practice and contradiction* (Revolutions) (London: Verso).

Marx, K. (1968 [1845]) 'Theses on Feuerbach', in K. Marx and F. Engels, *The German ideology* (Moscow: Progress), pp. 659–62.

— (1970 [1859]) *Contribution to the Critique of Political Economy*, trans. S.W. Ryazanskaya (Moscow: Progress).

— (1974 [1844]) *Economic and philosophic manuscripts of 1844* (Moscow: Progress).

— (1979 [1852]) *The Eighteenth Brumaire of Louis Bonaparte*, in *Collected Works*, Vol. 11 (Moscow: Progress).

Marx, K. and Engels, F. (1968 [1846]) *The German ideology* (Moscow: Progress).

Mayo, P. (1999) *Gramsci, Freire, and adult education: Possibilities for transformative action* (London: Zed).

iotant fy

Mojab, S. (2001) 'Theorizing the politics of "Islamic feminism"', *Feminist Review*, Vol. 69, 124–46.

— (2010) '(Re)theorizing and (Re)learning patriarchy', Lecture, 10 April, State College, PA: Pennsylvania State University.

Rikowski, G. (1996) 'Left alone: End time for Marxist educational theory?', *British Journal of Sociology of Education*, Vol. 17, No. 4, 415–51.

— (1997) 'Scorched earth: Prelude to rebuilding Marxist educational theory', *British Journal of Sociology of Education*, Vol. 18, No. 4, 551–74.

Sangari, K. (2015) 'Patriarchy/Patriarchies', in S. Mojab (ed.), *Marxism and Feminism*, (London: Zed), pp. 259–86.

Sayer, D. (1979) *Marx's method* (Atlantic Highlands: Humanities Press).

— (1987) *The violence of abstraction: The analytical foundations of historical materialism* (New York: Basil Blackwell).

Sekyi-Otu, A. (1996) *Fanon's dialectic of experience* (Cambridge, MA: Harvard University Press).

Shandro, A. (1995), '"Consciousness from without": Marxism, Lenin and the Proletariat', *Science and Society*, Vol. 59, No. 3, 268–97.

Smith, D.E. (1988) *The everyday world as problematic* (Toronto: University of Toronto Press).

— (1990) *The conceptual practices of power: A feminist sociology of knowledge* (Boston: Northeastern University Press).

— (2004) 'Ideology, science and social relations: A reinterpretation of Marx's epistemology', *European Journal of Social Theory*, Vol. 7, No. 4, 445–62.

Thomas, P.D. (2009) *The Gramscian moment* (Leiden: Koninklijke Brill).

Warminski, A. (1995) 'Hegel/Marx: Consciousness and life', *Yale French Studies*, Vol. 88, 118–41.

Wilde, O. (1994) 'The soul of man under socialism', in *The Complete Works of Oscar Wilde* (New York: HarperCollins), pp. 1174–97.

4

Centring Marxist Feminist Theory in Adult Learning

In recounting the mundane experiences of women during war, the poet Muriel Rukeyser asked a question that sits at the very centre of feminist praxis: 'What would happen if one woman told the truth about her life?' Her response: 'the world would split open' (Rukeyser, 2005, p. 463). The relation established in these quick stanzas troubles feminist educators; how to learn from the experiences of women – the experiences of violence, racism, sexism, poverty and exploitation – in order to 'split the world open'? There has been much debate amongst feminist scholars on how best to understand not only such a splitting of the world, or rather its transformation, but also the notion of learning that might sit at the centre of such a process. It is this theorization that is critical to the work of feminist educators. However, mirroring the debates within feminism, there is an important conflict between the kind of feminist theory employed in education and the critical tradition of education, particularly in regards to a critique of capitalist social relations, a vision of social transformation, and the political possibilities developed within our theoretical work. This tension is rooted in the long-standing philosophical debate concerning the relationship between the ideal and the material, but for adult educators these conversations in feminist theory have important implications for how we conceptualize several core elements of learning theory, particularly the individual, the social and experience. Here we consider these core relations of learning from a feminist-materialist perspective, drawing on post-structuralist examples for contrast and clarification, and chart a feminist direction for a Marxist feminist theory of adult learning.

Situating feminist materialism in adult education theory

Over the last 30 years, feminist scholars in adult education have made important and expansive critiques of the presuppositions of the field.

These interrogations have ranged from the questioning of patriarchal biases in the practices and theory of adult learning (Burke and Jackson, 2007; Flannery and Hayes, 2001; Hart, 1992; Hayes and Flannery, 2000; Sandlin, 2005; Thompson, 1983) to the development of feminist epistemologies, pedagogies and forms of resistance (Barr, 1999; Belenky et al., 1997; English, 2005, 2006; Ryan, 2001; Tisdell, 1993; Walters, 1996; Walters and Manicom, 1996). In many ways the work of feminist adult educators has echoed the ebb and flow of theoretical developments in feminist theory, which is largely characterized by a turn towards post-modern and post-structural theories emphasizing difference, identity, fragmentation and hybridity. In recent years, adult educators have gravitated towards this framework to theorize notions of gender, sexuality and patriarchy and the 'intersecting' social phenomena of gender, race, class, ability, age and so on in relation to adult learning and education. At the same time, feminist scholars across multiple disciplines continue to engage in important debates about the role of the material in our theorizations of various forms of social difference, oppression and knowledge (Ahmed, 2008; Ebert, 2005; Hennessy and Ingraham, 1997; Howe, 2010). These debates have made their way into adult education through the work of feminist educators who marry the post-structural emphasis on identity with the critical relations of political economy (Butterwick, 2008; Gouthro, 2005; Gouthro et al., 2002; Hart, 1992), particularly through utilizing critical theory and Habermasian frameworks.

These contributions are exceedingly important and have greatly expanded our understanding of how the social relations of gender, race, class, age, ability, nation and language form and inform the experiences of adult learners in a variety of social contexts. We want to argue, however, that a feminist-materialist framework, one which is explicitly a Marxist feminist approach, adds a necessary dimension to ongoing debates concerning the individual, the social, experience, learning and consciousness, debates which remain active in our field as we struggle against a pervasive, hyper-psychologized focus on the individual in the face of neoliberal reforms and the advance of an imperialist stage of capitalist development (Martin 2008; Mojab, 2006). It is our belief, following Dorothy E. Smith (1990), that a solution to this problem lies in utilizing theoretical tools that neither entrench the individual in abstract universalism nor detach them from the material and cultural relations of life (see Chapter 3).

Taking the position of Marxist feminism in adult education may seem an intriguing choice given the rejection of Marxism by prominent socialist feminist adult educators, such as Thompson (2000), and the popularity of post-structuralism as the basis of feminist epistemology and pedagogy (Tisdell, 1998). However, while many of the claims laid against Marx by feminist adult educators, particularly in relation to notions of ideology, consciousness and dualism, are understandable given the historical development of positivist political economy, they are unfounded when examined through the fully explicated framework of dialectical historical materialism advocated in this book, especially when we elaborate this framework through advances in feminist, anti-racist and anti-colonial theory. Paula Allman has persuasively argued for this position to the adult education community (1999, 2001, 2007). Further, the imperialist problems of militarism and monopoly capitalism, as well as the pervasive neoliberalization of the practices and policies of adult education, suggest that we utilize theoretical orientations that provide us with the ability to explain these phenomena in their fully contradictory appearances (Mojab, 2009).

Marxist feminism is, to us, not simply a set of theoretical constructs that we use to guide our interpretation of the world. It is a framework for inquiry, the production of knowledge and political struggle; it has provided a way of looking at how the social world and everyday/everynight experience is organized through the everyday activity of people and a way of understanding how certain forms of knowledge come to dominate not only our consciousness, but our activity and forms of social organization as well. Historically, Marxist theorizing in adult education has been mired in the debates concerning the determination between base and superstructure. It has followed the various twists and turns of Marxist and neo-Marxist theorizing that characterize the struggle of educators to understand the relationships between material life, consciousness and human agency (Rikowski, 1996). In embracing the analytic foundations of Marx, we argue that adult educators should work from a particular strain of Marxist theorizing, typically known as dialectical historical materialism, of which, for educators, the most important components are dialectical conceptualization and its application to understanding social relations, ideology and praxis (Allman, 2001, 2007). This strain of Marxist theorizing has a long history in adult education, notably in the foundational work of Freire and Vygotsky (Au 2007a, 2007b). What readers will find qualitatively different in dialectical readings of Marx is a deviation from the economic determinism of positivist political economy towards an emphasis on Marx's method. While this type of theorizing can be found in many important works, it is perhaps most clearly elaborated in the work of Marxist feminists who seek to explain the experience not just of capitalism, but of racism and patriarchy as well.

Through dialectical conceptualization, we revisit Marx and Engels' argument concerning the dangers of dichotomizing the ideal, our consciousness, and the material, our everyday existence. Understood dialectically, the ideal and the material exist in a mutually determining relation. This leads to a method of seeing social relationships as composed of mutually determining forces; opposites not necessarily in conflict per se, but which cannot develop outside of their relation to one another, a relation based in struggle and negation. The notion of dialectics is influenced by the Marxist feminist argument that social reality is best understood not as a structure or system but as human activity and forms of consciousness, as intricate forms of human social relations. In this way, we come to understand Marx and Engels' emphasis on the material world as a focus on the relations through which we produce and reproduce not just our physical existence, but our entire 'mode of life' (Marx and Engels, 1968, p. 32). This 'mode of life' encompasses not just economic production, but the ways in which we organize social relations to create that production and mediate our lives in order to reproduce them. In this way, Marxist feminists understand 'the material' to be socially organized through the social relations of gender and race, arguing that race and gender are not just cultural discourses, but 'no less than active social organization' (Bannerji, 1995, p. 149). Bannerji argues that race and gender are logics we use to organize our world, the ideas and knowledge we circulate, the ways in which we labour and produce. However, they are also actual human active sensuous practices, concretized in our activity and consciousness through ongoing *acts* of racialization and gendering. The social formations of race, gender and class are dialectically related social phenomena and cannot be disarticulated from one another, but rather continually shape and influence how our behaviour and consciousness of each develops and changes. Leopoldina Fortunati's (1995) and Silvia Federici's (2004) extensive analyses of the historical development of capitalism demonstrate how social practices of gendering and 'othering' are both *preconditions* for the development of the capitalist mode of production and its *results*. They argue that the material base of capitalism only developed because of its ability to take hold of and transform already existing social practices of difference and that these social relations constitute the social organization of the accumulation of capital. Thus, we understand sexism, racism and other forms of difference to be social practices historically specific to capitalism and so dialectically related with modes of consciousness that are historically specific as well. These forms of consciousness specific to capitalism are characterized by the predominance of ideology (Allman, 2007). Dialectical conceptualization of the ideal and the material gives rise to a critique of ideology as a method of thought, based in particular forms of abstraction that reify the social world outside of human activity, distorting our understanding of the relations of domination and exploitation that characterize our everyday lives (Smith, 2004). Ideology presents our everyday experience in an upside-down fashion, making reality appear as if meaning, language and materiality are divorced from one another. This separation is a central focus of Marxist feminist critique.

Marxist feminist theory offers a radically different articulation of difference and experience than the concepts of 'interlocking' or 'intersecting' forms of oppression. This difference is located in an ontology grounded in dialectical historical materialism, although some recent applications of Marxist feminism in the field of adult education (Gouin, 2009) have divorced Marxist feminism from this grounding. Marxist feminists have counterposed themselves to post-modern, post-structural, structural and liberal feminists by explicitly rejecting a separation between the realm of ideas and the world of the material. At the centre of this project is a re-theorization of the material as a necessarily sexed and gendered and differenced human phenomenon existing in a dialectical relationship with forms of consciousness. Thus, from the perspective of Marxist feminist educators we do not study the social world as the circulation of representations and discourses, but as an active human project of historically organized social practices, relations and forms of consciousness. Feminist scholars in our field are already developing this analysis by examining educational practices such as lifelong learning (Colley, 2002; Mojab, 2009), informal learning (Gorman, 2007), citizenship learning (Carpenter, 2009), and learning in the Diaspora and under conditions of war (Mojab and Gorman, 2003; Gorman and Mojab, 2008).

Feminist readings of the individual–social–experience relation in educational theory

As Tisdell (1998) has demonstrated, various feminist models have found favour with adult educators. First, feminist educators have focused on the individual or the psychologized models of feminism found in the famous *Women's Ways of Knowing* texts (Belenky et al., 1997). In reaction to this emphasis on the individual, the focus shifted to structural models, whose theorists were subsequently accused of negating human agency by making individuals victims of social structures and systems. In a similar move, feminist educators largely rejected the conservative post-modern denunciation of truth and agency for its profound limitations in theorizing feminist and anti-racist struggle. Feminists across the social sciences have popularized post-structuralism because of its proposed solution to the individual–social problem, particularly its emphasis on the connections between the individual and the social. These connections are fleshed out in the notion of positionality, or the idea that one's subject location is found at the intersection of multiple, shifting identities. The implications of this argument in adult education have been a noted increase in scholarship that emphasizes the issue of the positionality of the instructor or adult educator. Our purpose here is not to argue that the question of positionality is an unimportant or trivial project for adult educators. Rather, it is important to interrogate where the post-structuralist notion of positionality comes from and what its implications are as an analytic tool for feminist adult education practice. How we theorize the relationship between the individual and the social has important implications for what constitutes the experience of the connection between them and thus of learning. Only then do we know what it means to be 'positioned'. In what follows, our purpose is not to provide an overarching critique of post-structuralist feminism, but rather to examine the extension of its arguments into adult learning.

As will be familiar to many, part of the theoretical base of post-structural feminism is the notion of discursive construction. In this framework, what is of the utmost importance is the deconstruction, often through historical inquiry, of the various representations, discourses and signifiers that characterize our social practices, consciousness and history – and which find their realization in language (Palmer, 1990). With this project in mind, post-structural theory compels us to interact with the social world as a historical arrangement of discursive representations in which the individual, the subject, is caught up in processes of making and unmaking, domination and resistance, othering and defining, and constant change. Translated back into the practice of adult education, the individual, as subject, is in fact positioned within these overlapping and contradictory discourses. Their identity as an individual is constructed and named through these discourses, and the work of adult education is then to deconstruct and rename; thus our pedagogical emphasis on naming identities, opposing binaries and essentialization, and claiming knowledge from these previously, and contemporarily, marginalized locations. Mojab (2009) has argued that this processes of naming only partially explains the social reality confronted by adult learners. If the social is understood as a cadre of complicated discursive constructions, and the individual is the subject whose identity is both determined and resisted within those discourses, then the notion of experience follows in a logically manner. Joan Scott, in a popular argument, encapsulated the position in this way:

> Subjects are constituted discursively, but there are conflicts among discursive systems, contradictions within any one of them, multiple meanings possible for the concepts they deploy. And subjects have agency. They are not unified, autonomous individuals exercising free will, but rather subjects whose agency is created through situations and statuses conferred to them. Being a subject means being 'subject to definite conditions of existence, conditions of endowment of agents and conditions of exercise' ... Subjects are constituted discursively, experience is a linguistic event (it doesn't happen outside established meanings), but neither is it confined to a fixed order of meaning. Since discourse is by definition shared, experience is collective as well as individual. Experience is a subject's history. Language is the site of history's enactment. Historical explanation cannot, therefore, separate the two. The question then becomes how to analyse language. (1992, p. 34)

An important point made here is the notion that experience does not 'happen outside established meanings'. This is an embodiment of the essentially post-modern notion that reality, objectivity, does not exist outside of individual interpretive processes, or rather that 'there is no escaping what theorists call the hermeneutic circle' (Michelson, 1996, p. 190). If the individual is a discursively constituted subject, the social is the circulation of discourses, and experience is constituted through our shared meanings, representations and discourses, then we arrive at the question of language. Positionality, as a pedagogical analytic, then becomes the interrogation of discourses, the reflection and projection of meanings onto the subject. It also becomes an epistemological claim of access to those discourses and the experiences that are constituted through them. For post-structuralist feminist pedagogues, these are the experiences that sit at the centre of feminist pedagogical praxis.

In order to flesh out this position, let us take, as an example, the proposal for situated knowledge as an epistemological basis for a feminist adult education theory and practice (Michelson, 1996). To clarify, situated knowledge is not the same thing as situated cognition or situated learning. These latter terms are familiar to adult educators and are typically used to refer to sociocultural theories of context-based learning. For feminist adult educators, however, situated knowledge has become a theoretical tool for addressing the question of the relationship between the individual and the social in learning and knowledge production. In this sense, situated knowledge is an attempt by feminist scholars to carve out a space for feminist objectivity (Haraway, 1988). The assertion is that knowledge is based in positionality and that the knowledge of the subjugated, produced through experiences of oppression, is privileged in its ability to unmask the relations of domination that characterize society and to see beyond the infinite vision, 'the god trick', of the objectified universal subject. The insistence is that all knowledge, all seeing, is partial, local, grounded, subjective, and specific. Experience in this arrangement is the position from which the subjugated 'see', remembering that experience is discursively organized and mediated.

Haraway adds two important and interrelated caveats to the argument for situated knowledge, both of which are particularly significant in relation to how the thesis has played out in adult education. First, the positionality of knowledge means that one must be very careful not to attempt a false embodiment of the subjugated in claiming to see from their position; hence, our emphasis on positionality in the classroom and voice and perspective in research. Second, the danger remains that the subjugated can be fetishized and romanticized and their 'sight' digested uncritically by those around them. Haraway argued that 'the positions of the subjugated are not exempt from critical re-examination, decoding, deconstruction, and interpretation: that is, from both semiological and hermeneutic modes of critical inquiry' (1988, p. 584). We can see here that in the argument for situated knowledge, we have come full circle within an ontology and epistemology of discourse. The knowing subject produces knowledge from their position about the social discursive constructions of their own subject position. That knowledge is then subjected to modes of inquiry that deconstruct the discourses and knowledges that have framed the hermeneutic of experience in the first place. Armed with new knowledge of the discursive construction of their subject position, the knowing subject is now able to mount a resistance against othering subjectivities and the institutionalized cultural signifiers of various forms of oppression. She or he is ready to do battle, as Marx and Engels put it, with 'the phrases of the world' (1968, p. 30).

This battle is an important political project. The problem for critical adult educators is that the outcome of adult education might not simply be a changed consciousness or new modes of interpretation, but also the radical and revolutionary reorganization of our mode of life. The goal extends beyond understanding our oppression and towards its material transformation. The disagreement, however, is not just in what the outcomes should be. The argument we are making is that analytical tools help us to see different political possibilities through the way in which they describe and explain our daily lives. For us, the political aspirations of post-structuralist feminist educators are necessary, but they are not adequate. As Himani Bannerji (1995) has argued, it is true that the history and experience of domination creates the need to negate the identity it forms. However, resistance to that imposition implies more than negation through discursive constructions. It also projects a new history. What is compelling about the argument for situated knowledge is the idea of power, authority and voice that can be claimed through such a position. However, knowledge is always local and partial because it is shaped by the particular discursive constellation in which it exists, unable to connect a common materiality to its formation. Is power condemned to these limits as well? Capital most certainly is not. As identified by many critical feminist educators, here the politics of post-structuralism come to a crossroads with critical adult education. How can we craft a basis for mobilization if all experience is local and knowledge is privileged to situated subject positions? It is for this reason that Marxist feminist scholars and educators have attempted to chart a re-imagined notion of experience, one that places active social relations at its centre.

For Marx, the problem of the individual and the social is intricately connected to the debate between idealism and various forms of materialism as philosophical frameworks. Briefly, Marx rejected idealist philosophy, which posits that human consciousness dictates social reality. Stated another way, he objected to the notion that the world we live in is exclusively the product of the ideas we have, the language we use to describe it, or the meaning we attribute to it – or, in other words, discourses that circulate above the ground. The genius of *The German Ideology* is to have demonstrated that the exact opposite of idealism – a crude, deterministic materialist philosophy that argues that reality dictates consciousness – is in fact a replication of idealism. For both of these perspectives, reality is only considered as '*the object of contemplation*, but not as *sensuous human activity, practice*, not subjectively' (Marx, 1968, p. 659, emphasis in the original). Marx and Engels argued that their peers were thinking about social reality as merely forms of consciousness that exist outside of people; or, in the language of adult educators, as knowledge or culture that is objectified outside the learner or as 'social forces' that condition or contextualize learning. Marx argued that social reality is human activity; the social world is made up of all the labours we perform in co-operation with one another *and* the way we think and make meaning out of this work. The relationship between reality and consciousness is not linear, but dialectical, and thus the relationship between the individual and the social is not static or external, but internal (Allman, 2001). By this we mean that if the social world is composed of our activity, then we cannot be separated from it. We are always active participants in the everyday world around us. This is not a rejection of discourse per se; rather, it is a rejection of the artificial separation of discourse and human activity whereby discourse, objectified human consciousness, is understood as having an existence independent of active human practice. If this were indeed the case, we would only 'have to fight against these illusions of consciousness. Since according to their [the Young Hegelians'] fantasy, the relationships of men [*sic*], all their doings, their chains and their limitations are products of consciousness' (Marx and Engels, 1968, p. 30). But as adult educators, we know this not to be the case. Post-structuralist feminists also know this not to be the case, particularly the post-structural materialist feminists, who struggle to reconcile the deconstruction of the discourses of gender and the resistance of 'micro-powers' with the continued violent exploitation of women by capital. This moment of atrophy can be found in the explanatory limits of a theoretical framework that disarticulates people from their own labour, their own thinking, their own messy, convoluted lives.

Marx's notion of the social very clearly encompasses the total relations and organization of collective life. Often this notion of the social is understood as 'material', but is reduced to the economic. Marx and Engels' explicitly counter this interpretation when they argue that 'this mode of production must not be considered simply as being the production of the physical existence of the individuals. Rather it is a definite form of activity of these individuals, a definite form of expressing their life, a definite *mode of life* on their part' (1968, p. 32, emphasis in the original). For Marx and Engels, the notion of the material is inherently social and the social is inherently material. The ways in which we organize our collective life to produce the world are bound up in complex forms of human relations. It is particularly crucial that feminist adult educators understand that the notion of social and material relations expressed by Marx and Engels is not an argument for the centrality or determinism of the economic or even of production. This is because the social and the material are also historical. This argument has been more clearly fleshed out by Bannerji (1995), who has also complicated the concept of social relations of capitalism by demonstrating how these relations are necessarily gendered and othered. The social, contrary to the notion of discursive circulation, is understood as a mass of complex, complicated, dialectical relations: 'I assume "the social" to mean a complex socioeconomic and cultural formation, brought to life through myriad finite and specific social and historical relations, organizations, and institutions. It involves living and conscious human agents in what Marx called their "sensuous, practical human activity"' (1995, p. 146).

What should be emerging here is a picture of the social world in which we act within the meaning we attribute to our experiences in very specific ways; this is a relationship in which meaning and social organization mutually determine one another. Further, we can see that individuals are understood here not just as agents of discursive relations alone, but as 'conscious human agents' and organizers of social life.

What is also apparent is the difference between Joan Scott's notion of the individual–social relation and the relation forged in dialectical historical materialism. There is an important difference between, on the one hand, conceiving of the world as composed solely of forms of consciousness that dictate social practice and, on the other hand, pursuing a notion of the dialectical relationships of consciousness and practice (that is, praxis) and of the individual and the social. The difference is the distance between being able to describe conditions of exploitation, domination and oppression and being able to explain them in terms of mutually determining relations between how we think about something and how we act. For example, the condition of women in low-wage work around the world is an actual practice of labour exploitation that results in a violent experience of poverty and which is endemic and necessary to the accumulation of capital. Our understanding, our consciousness, of labour is that women's labour, specifically the labour of women of colour, is less valuable in capitalist production. This understanding is a result not just of the fact that this ideology permeates our daily reality, but also because we actually organize labour and accumulation on this ideology; we act as if it is true. This is the mutually determining, dialectical relation of praxis.

A Marxist feminist approach to the dialectical relation of the individual and the social world implies a radically different notion of experience. Feminist adult educators have critiqued the traditional theorization of experience in adult education for its reliance on a masculinist notion of rationality (Michelson, 1996). As highlighting the limitations of Enlightenment epistemologies, these critiques are important, but we want to propose that something deeper is occurring which has gone unaddressed by the notion of experience as a linguistic and hermeneutic event. We want to propose that in the field of adult education we have largely relied on a reified notion of experience as the basis for a theory of learning. By reification we do not mean commodification; this is a relationship that has been profoundly misunderstood in our field. By reification we mean, simply, 'mistaking abstract concepts for real entities' (Sayer, 1987, p. 54; see also Chapter 3, above). This is part of the epistemological process Marx identified as ideology, which is often taken to simply mean a system of ideas, or that knowledge is produced through abstraction. In this mistake lies the feminist critique of Marx's epistemic rationality. It is worth pointing out that the fact that all knowledge relies on abstraction does not, in turn, mean that all abstractions are based in reason or even in science or any sense of objectivity or subjectivity. Even the deconstructing of discourse relies on abstraction. Abstraction itself is not necessarily the problem; rather, the manner of the abstraction is. In this way, adult educators have reified experience because we have theorized it as an abstraction from an abstraction; we have posited it as a static entity that is an experience *of* the world and not *in* the world, certainly not in a world of our own collective historical making. The post-structural solution to this problem is to posit experience as the experience of language, or as people framing who you are through the ways in which they describe you. But that is not all that happens. It is for this reason that Marx and Engels argue that 'the premises from which we begin are not arbitrary ones ... they are the real individuals, their activity and the material conditions under which they live, both those which they find already existing and those produced by their activity' (1968, p. 31).

If we follow a Marxist feminist ontology, then 'experience' is our participation in disjointed social relations (Smith, 1988). As such, we do not attempt to understand experience as a pre-reflective, sensory driven phenomenon or only as the movement of meanings. Instead, we focus on the 'particular historical forms of social relations that determine that experience' (Smith, 1988, p. 49). In this way, we move beyond understanding 'the ideas, images, and symbols in which our experience is given social form as that neutral floating thing called culture' (p. 54). Instead, we focus on how we construct knowledge from our experience in relation to delineating the historical and material relations that condition it and which constitute our social world. From a Marxist feminist perspective, the notion of experience must consider the complexity of these material appearances and forms. This is something that as adult educators we have struggled to do, and have recently fallen back on notions of subjectivity and difference to understand experience. But, as Bannerji has argued, 'social subjectivities' are not a 'found object on the ground of ontology, nor are they to be seen only as functions of discourses' (2001, p. 3). By this Bannerji is referring to Marxist epistemology in that individuals and their practice in the world are the embodiment of the dialectical relationship between forms of consciousness and the active human social relations that make up our everyday experience. Further, these social relations are understood to have both a universal and a particular character. This is contrary to the notion that all experience, and thus all knowledge, is local and partial. While we are not arguing that knowledge is infinite, we are agreeing with these Marxist feminist scholars who search for a base in theory that can describe, explain and transform the experiences of oppression that drive learning in the first place. For these scholars, experience must be situated with a historical analysis of capitalist social relations in order to engage in resistance and transformation.

To make the claim that all of our experiences take place within definite historical social relations is to claim a kind of universality for them. By that we mean that we all live within the historical relations of the capitalist mode of production. Even those of us who live on the periphery of that form of production live within a world characterized by its inner logic. This claim, however, is not a continuation of the long history of economic determinism associated with positivist forms of political economy. We are rejecting any notion that 'class', understood mechanistically or simply, is the basis of all forms of oppression. Determinism, either of the economic or cultural sort, will not do, although they are extremely seductive positions. Even the most sophisticated of Marxist feminist scholars, such as Ebert (1996, 2005), struggle to theorize their way out of a rigid reading of materialism. To substitute one for the other has proven a false direction. Rather, as Marxist feminists, we understand forms of oppression to be bound up with each other and mutually determined with the social relations of capitalism. This is not to say that patriarchy or racism did not exist before capitalism. It is clear from the historical research of scholars such as Silvia Federici (2004) that capitalism could not have developed without gender and difference, specifically race, as social practices. Rather, we argue that history conditions our experience of these forms of oppression. In advanced capitalist democracies, we do not experience patriarchy as women did under feudalism; although feudal and capitalist forms of patriarchy exist in many societies today (Bannerji, Mojab and Whitehead, 2001). Colonialism, the historical period of capitalist expansion, and imperialism, its current period of development, characterize our understandings of racial difference (see Chapter 6). By this we mean that race is sexed, gendered and classed, class is sexed, gendered and raced, sex and gender are classed and raced, and so on. This understanding of difference is inherent to a Marxist feminist understanding of experience. In contrast, Donna Haraway, a foundational theorist of situated knowledge, has argued that 'There is no way to "be" simultaneously in all, or wholly in any, of the privileged (i.e. subjugated) positions structured by gender, race, nation, and class … The search for such a "full" and total position is the search for the fetishized perfect subject of oppositional history' (1988, p. 586). Bannerji (1995) has argued the opposite. It is impossible to disarticulate these social relations from one another without objectifying the social and artificially separating relations of oppression from each another through a cultural logic that segments race and gender from capital and class. Again, we return to the problem of theorizing the social as something other than historically subjective human practice. To be clear, this is a radically different notion of difference and experience than the popular frameworks of intersectionality and positionality.

Advancing a feminist-materialist theory of learning

Advancing a theory of learning from a feminist-materialist and Marxist feminist position requires three interrelated intellectual projects. First, and most obvious, is to develop a rigorous, historical and scientific understanding of the circulation and accumulation of capital and its constituent social relations that compose the daily experience of adult learners. Second, in order to understand these relations, our experience and forms of consciousness and their transformation, we must deeply explore Marxist notions of dialectics, contradiction and negation. Third, we must continue the work of multiple scholars who have engaged the question of ideology, but expand this work by discussing ideology not only as content, but as an epistemology and thus a pedagogical practice. Feminist scholars in adult education have taken great and extensive pains to document the many different ways in which women learn in varied social and political contexts. What we often forget in all of this documentation is that the learning we are describing in feminist accounts is not 'learning' per se, learning abstracted, learning differentiated, although this is how we name it. This 'learning' is a historically specific mode of coming to know the world around one, based in the ideological forms and appearances of capitalist social relations. We experience the world as fractured, disconnected, non-linear; the ways in which we (un)learn this world appear to be the same. This is not evidence of what 'learning' is; this is evidence of learning in a capitalist, patriarchal, racist, heterosexist world. The efforts by Marxist feminist educators to revise our notion of adult learning are not limited to reworking our theoretical paradigms for the purposes of new descriptions of social phenomena. Rather, a Marxist feminist notion of adult learning pushes us to consider the relationship between active social organization, re-organization and learning; while consciousness moves in unconscious ways, the outcome of educational efforts will not be just new ways to make meaning, but also transformed human relations and practice.

The critique of ideology as pedagogical practice begs the question of Marxist feminist methods of practice. At this point in the development of Marxist feminist theory in adult education, it would be premature to be prescriptive about pedagogical methods. It is apparent that the argument we have made here implies a strong role for the educator and for under-standing education as purposeful, intentional pedagogic intervention. We have always gravitated towards the notion of the two-eyed teacher found in Myles Horton's (1990) work and to his articulation of the dual character of teaching. As educators, we begin with everyday experience and consciousness; for lack of better terminology, we work from where the learner is 'at'. At the same time, our role as educators is to challenge and interrogate, and to ensure that learning is an active process of change and negation, corresponding to the actual forms and practices of social life. Only in this way can the constant potential of Marx's humanism be fulfilled.

Moving forward it is important to develop Marxist feminist pedagogy through the theory of revolutionary praxis. While there is much overlap and similarity in intent and processes across feminist pedagogical projects, and the interrogation of experience remains the central epistemological project of adult education, the revolutionary notion of praxis implies a few re-orientations on the part of adult educators. Reflection cannot stop at the acknowledgement of shared experience and cannot fast forward to political action. Analysis has to go beyond experience itself and into the social conditions that determine experience and the forms of conscious-ness we have used to interpret our experience. These conditions and our relation to them have to be interrogated as a source of knowledge, and the conditions have to be historicized and understood as relations. If race is the salient characteristic of the experience, our reflection must expand beyond race to 'race in relation' in order to have a dialectical articulation of race. This means that feminist educators have to reject the anti-theory orientation of pragmatism. Critical praxis requires abstraction not just of what we think, but also of how we think. This is the intellectual method of revolutionary praxis; the critical theorization of the self.

In conclusion and to summarize, a feminist-materialist theory of adult learning, a Marxist feminist theory, will begin with a completely revised notion of the individual, the social and experience drawn from a feminist and anti-racist extension of dialectical historical materialism. This ontology is a dialectical historical materialist one in which the social is posited as sensuous human practice and people as the historical agents of their own world. We want to emphasize in advancing a Marxist feminist theory of adult learning that it is just as important to pay attention to forms of consciousness as to social organization and practice. Discourse is important. It is important to recognize that our attractions to this notion of the social, particularly as educators, are understandable. These ideas provide insight into the very visceral experience of oppression. However, in embracing them to the exclusion of the material, we undermine our own ability to go beyond and outside, to split open, the world we have received from the past. We deny history, our own imaginative capacities, and the possibility of an active re-organization of both our consciousness and our collective social life.

References

Ahmed, S. (2008) 'Some preliminary remarks on the founding gestures of the "new materialism"', *European Journal of Women's Studies*, Vol. 15, No. 1, 23–39.

Allman, P. (1999) *Revolutionary social transformation: Democratic hopes, political possibilities and critical education* (Westport, CT: Bergin & Garvey).

— (2001) *Critical education against global capitalism: Karl Marx and revolutionary critical education* (Westport, CT: Bergin & Garvey).

— (2007) *On Marx: An introduction to the revolutionary intellect of Karl Marx* (Rotterdam: Sense).

Au, W. (2007a) 'Epistemology of the oppressed: The dialectics of Paulo Freire's theory of knowledge', *Journal of Critical Education Policy Studies*, Vol. 5, No. 2. Available at http://www.jceps.com/archives/551.

— (2007b) 'Vygotsky and Lenin on learning: The parallel structures of individual and social development', *Science and Society*, Vol. 71, No. 3, 273–98.

Bannerji, H. (1995) *Thinking through: Essays on feminism, Marxism, and anti-racism* (Toronto: Women's Press).

— (2001) *Inventing subjects: Studies in hegemony, patriarchy, and colonialism* (New Delhi: Tulika).

— (2011) 'Building from Marx: Reflections on "race", gender, and class', in S. Carpenter and S. Mojab (eds), *Educating from Marx: Race, gender, and learning* (New York: Palgrave Macmillan), pp. 41–62.

Bannerji, H., Mojab, S. and Whitehead, J. (eds) (2001) *Of property and propriety: The role of gender and class in imperialism and nationalism* (Toronto: University of Toronto Press).

Barr, J. (1999) *Liberating knowledge: Research, feminism, and adult education* (Leicester: NIACE).

Belenky, M.F., Clinchy, B.M., Goldberger, N.R and Tarule, J.M. (1997) *Women's ways of knowing* (New York: Basic Books).

Burke, P.J. and Jackson, S. (2007) *Re-conceptualizing lifelong learning* (London: Routledge).

Butterwick, S. (2008) 'Lessons of gender politics from the centre and the fringes of the knowledge-based society', in D. Livingstone, K. Mirchandani and P. Sawchuk (eds), *The future of lifelong learning and work: Critical perspectives* (Rotterdam: Sense), pp. 107–18.

Carpenter, S. (2009) 'Interrogating the call to service: The social relations of learning citizenship', in P. Coare and L. Cecil (eds), *Really useful research: Proceedings from the Standing Conference on University Teaching and Research in the Education of Adults* (Brighton: University of Sussex), pp. 81–8.

Colley, H. (2002) 'A rough guide to the history of mentoring from a Marxist feminist perspective', *Journal of Education for Teaching*, Vol. 28, 257–73.

Ebert, T.L. (1996) *Ludic feminism and after: Postmodernism, desire, and labor in late capitalism* (Ann Arbor: University of Michigan Press).

— (2005) 'Rematerializing feminism', *Science and Society*, Vol. 69, No. 1, 33–55.

English, L.M. (2005) 'Third-space practitioners: Women educating for justice in the Global South', *Adult Education Quarterly*, Vol. 55, No. 2, 85–100.

— (2006) 'A Foucauldian reading of learning in feminist, nonprofit organizations', *Adult Education Quarterly*, Vol. 56, No. 2, 85–101.

Federici, S. (2004) *Caliban and the witch: Women, the body, and primitive accumulation* (New York: Autonomedia).

Flannery, D.D. and Hayes, E. (2001) 'Challenging adult learning: A feminist perspective', in V. Sheared and P. Sissel (eds), *Making space: Merging theory and practice in adult education* (Santa Barbara: Greenwood), pp. 29–41.

Fortunati, L. (1995) *The arcane of reproduction: Housework, prostitution, labor, and capital*, trans. H. Creek (New York: Autonomedia).

Gorman, R. (2007) 'The feminist standpoint and the trouble with "informal learning": A way forwards for Marxist-feminist educational research', in A. Green, G. Rikowski and H. Raduntz (eds), *Renewing dialogues in Marxism and Education: Openings* (New York: Palgrave Macmillan), pp. 183–99.

Gorman, R. and Mojab, S. (2008) 'War, diaspora, learning, and women's standpoint', in M. Hajdukowski-Ahmed, N. Khanlou and H. Moussa (eds), *Not born a refugee woman: Contesting identities, rethinking practices* (New York: Berghahn), pp. 135–49.

Gouin, R. (2009) 'An anti-racist feminist analysis for the study of learning in social struggle', *Adult Education Quarterly*, Vol. 59, No. 2, 158–75.

Gouthro, P. (2005) 'A critical feminist analysis of the homeplace as learning site: Expanding the discourse of lifelong learning', *International Journal of Lifelong Education*, Vol. 24, No. 1, 5–19.

Gouthro, P., Miles, A., Butterwick, S., Fenwick, T. and Mojab, S. (2002) 'Five feminists: Perspectives on public policy and adult education', in *Adult education and the contested terrain of public policy*, Proceedings of the 21st Annual Conference of the Canadian Association for the Study of Adult Education (Toronto, ON: OISE/University of Toronto), pp. 408–14.

Haraway, D. (1988) 'Situated knowledges: The science question in feminism and the privilege of partial perspectives', *Feminist Studies*, Vol. 14, No. 3, 575–99.

Hart, M.U. (1992) *Working and educating for life: Feminism and international perspectives on adult education* (London: Routledge).

Hayes, E. and Flannery, D.D. (2000) *Women as learners: The significance of gender in adult learning* (San Francisco: Jossey-Bass).

Hennessy, R. and Ingraham, C. (eds) (1997) *Materialist feminism: A reader in class, difference, and women's lives* (New York: Routledge).

Horton, M. (1990) *The long haul: An autobiography* (New York: Teacher's College Press).

Howe, G. (2010) *Between feminism and materialism: A question of method* (New York: Palgrave Macmillan).

Martin, I. (2008) 'Whither adult education in the learning paradigm? Some personal reflections'. Plenary address to the 38th Annual SCUTREA Conference, 2–4 July 2008, University of Edinburgh. Available at www.scutrea.ac.uk.

Marx, K. (1968 [1845]) 'Theses on Feuerbach', in K. Marx and F. Engels, *The German Ideology* (Moscow: Progress), pp. 659–62.

Marx, K. and Engels, F. (1968 [1846]) *The German ideology*, trans S. Ryazanskaya (Moscow: Progress).

Michelson, E. (1996) 'Beyond Galileo's telescope', *Adult Education Quarterly*, Vol. 46, No. 4, 185–96.

Mojab, S. (2006) 'Adult education without borders', in T. Fenwick, T. Nesbit and B. Spencer (eds), *Contexts of adult education: Canadian perspectives* (Toronto: Thompson Educational), pp. 347–55.

— (2009) 'Learning by dispossession: Gender, imperialism, and adult education', in R.P. Lawrence (ed.), *Honoring our past, embracing our future*, Proceedings of the Adult Education Research Conference (Chicago, IL: National Louis University), pp. 242–7.

Mojab, S. and Gorman, R. (2003) 'Women and consciousness in the "learning organization": Emancipation or exploitation?' *Adult Education Quarterly*, Vol. 53, No. 4, 228–41.

Palmer, B. (1990) *Descent into discourse: The reification of language and the writing of social history* (Philadelphia: Temple University Press).

Rikowski, G. (1996) 'Left alone: End time for Marxist educational theory?', *British Journal of Sociology of Education*, Vol. 17, No. 4, 415–51.

Rukeyser, M. (2005) 'Kathe Kollwitz', in J.E. Kaufman and A.F. Herzog (eds), *The collected poems of Muriel Rukeyser* (Pittsburgh: University of Pittsburgh Press).

Ryan, A.B. (2001) *Feminist ways of knowing: Towards theorising the person for radical adult education* (Leicester: NIACE).

Sandlin, J. (2005) 'Andragogy and its discontents: An analysis of andragogy from three critical perspectives', *PAACE Journal of Lifelong Learning*, Vol. 14, 25–42.

Sayer, D. (1987) *The violence of abstraction: The analytical foundations of historical materialism* (New York: Basil Blackwell).

Scott, J.W. (1992) 'Experience', in J. Butler and J.W. Scott (eds), *Feminists theorize the political* (New York: Routledge), pp. 23–40.

Smith, D.E. (1988) *The everyday world as problematic* (Toronto: University of Toronto Press).

— (1990) *The conceptual practices of power: A feminist sociology of knowledge* (Boston: Northeastern University Press).

— (2004) 'Ideology, science and social relations: A reinterpretation of Marx's epistemology', *European Journal of Social Theory*, Vol. 7, No. 4, 445–62.

Thompson, J.L. (1983) *Learning liberation: Women's response to men's education* (London: Croom Helm).

— (2000) *Women, class, and education* (London: Routledge).

Tisdell, E.J. (1993) 'Feminism and adult learning: Power, pedagogy, and praxis', *New Directions for Adult and Continuing Education*, Vol. 57, 91–103.

— (1998) 'Post-structural feminist pedagogies: The possibilities and limitations of feminist emancipatory adult learning theory and practice', *Adult Education Quarterly*, Vol. 48, No. 3, 139–56.

Walters, S. (1996) 'Gender and adult education: Training gender-sensitive and feminist adult educators in South Africa – an emerging curriculum', in P. Wangoola and F. Youngman (eds), *Towards a transformative political economy of adult education: Theoretical and practical challenges* (DeKalb, IL: LEPS), pp. 293–320.

Walters, S. and Manicom, L. (eds) (1996) *Gender in popular education: Methods for empowerment* (London: CACE Publications and Zed Books).

5

Institutional Ethnography:
A Marxist Feminist Analysis

In this chapter we offer some theoretical explications for adapting the feminist sociological tool of institutional ethnography to the field of education. We emphasize that we are advocating for an explicitly Marxist feminist reading of institutional ethnography, in contradistinction to other readings of the method that de-emphasize or confuse its materialist-feminist ontology. For us, Marxist feminism offers analytical tools grounded in dialectical historical materialism with the ability to illuminate the inter-constitutive gendered and racialized social relations within capitalism. Furthermore, Marxist feminism calls us to collective struggle to transform these relations and thus to forms of research that will help to build the knowledge necessary for revolutionary struggle. We see institutional ethnography as a method that can re-emphasize dialectical historical materialism within critical education, advance the feminist and anti-racist analysis within our field, and actualize research into consciousness and learning for the purposes of revolutionary struggle.

Institutional ethnography, as developed by feminist sociologist Dorothy E. Smith, aims to reorganize 'the social relations of knowledge of the social' (Smith, 2005, p. 29), meaning the goals of institutional ethnography are not simply to produce knowledge on a given subject, but also to reorient our ways of thinking about social reality and how it can be known. While Smith's work has had a significant international influence in women's studies and sociology, it has been far less used by critical educational theorists, with a few notable exceptions in the field of adult education (Carpenter, 2011; Grahame, 1998; Gruner, 2012; Jackson, 1995; Ng 1988, 1995; Wilmot, 2011). Our assertion here is that institutional ethnography, as an approach to social inquiry that actualizes a Marxist feminist ontology, is essential to the development of a Marxist feminist analysis of consciousness, learning and praxis.

Institutional ethnography (IE) is a method of inquiry that actualizes the ontology and epistemology developed by Marx and Engels in *The German Ideology* (1968 [1846]) and offers us an empirical method for discovering the processes of praxis and consciousness in the everyday organization of learning and social relations. In what follows, we will situate IE within the broader field of research into consciousness in educational scholarship, expand on our understanding of IE as an approach to inquiry, and conclude with some insights into how IE can be utilized by revolutionary scholars and activists.

Critical educational inquiry into consciousness/praxis

Educational researchers working in the critical tradition have developed a variety of approaches to empirically describing and establishing the characteristics of the learning associated with processes of politicization or, as normally described, conscientization. Beyond the field of critical pedagogy and its focus on cultural forms, critical education researchers have been primarily interested in the various kinds of learning, including non-political forms, that emerge from participation in social struggle and social movements (Choudry, 2015; Foley, 1999; Hall et al., 2011), as well as the processes of critical consciousness raising associated with modes of popular education and participatory action research (PAR), including feminist and youth participatory action research as well as community-based participatory research (Cammarota and Fine, 2008; Kapoor and Jordan, 2009; McIntyre, 2008). Since the emergence of PAR in the 1970s, it has become something of the status quo of methodological approaches to studying the development of critical consciousness, although phenomenological, ethnographic, life history, critical discourse analysis and ethno-methodological approaches are also frequently used. Transformative learning theories, both those associated with Mezirow (1991, 2000) and O'Sullivan (1999), have also produced research around 'critical consciousness', although Mezirow's perspective-shift framework is perhaps the most fully realized psychological approach to the question. Similarly, the study of consciousness has been taken up through the perspective of social movement learning, which became caught up in late twentieth-century debates concerning new versus old social movements (Holst, 2011).

Perhaps of more significance than the approach to data collection has been the particular epistemologies and ontologies deployed by researchers that guide their conceptualization of what learning 'is' and what it 'looks like' in politicized processes. A guiding assumption of this diverse field is that through participation or engagement in some process of social contestation, new forms of consciousness can and do emerge. A major difficulty for researchers has been dealing with problems of categorizing some forms of consciousness as 'false' or 'critical', thus demonstrating a lack of differentiation between a formulation of consciousness per se and class consciousness as a collective expression of praxis (Ollman, n.d.). The danger here is to reduce consciousness and praxis to its thought content, rather than the epistemological position we have advocated in this book (see Chapter 4). This reduction can only be addressed through an emphasis on the relationship between human practice and forms of consciousness. There are various ways to address this necessity, one of which is through attention to *human activity*.

In recent years, Cultural Historical Activity Theory (CHAT) has emerged as a framework for the exploration of critical learning, primarily in workplace settings (Engeström, 2001; Sawchuk, Duarte and Elhammoumi, 2006). CHAT has attracted educators working in critical traditions in part because of its claims to accounting for processes of learning, change and struggle. Within the CHAT framework, the primary object of analysis is an activity system that is assumed to be social, or collective, in nature, oriented towards material conditions and processes, mediated through artefacts, and involving historicity. Activity systems evolve through human practice and contain multiple contradictions, which are seen to drive change and development within the activity system. These contradictions within activity systems can cause more profound agitation, leading to potential transformation, wherein some individuals may orient themselves in opposition to the system, thus leading to possibilities for collaboration, learning and struggle, ultimately generating new activity systems and new forms of knowledge. CHAT draws heavily from traditions within Marxism, in particular Vygotsky, aimed at developing a materialist social psychology that understands individual consciousness as embedded within social relations and forms of social consciousness. Changes in objective conditions that are present in activity systems are understood to be a means to overcome forms of alienation and produce changes in consciousness.

CHAT has been subject to some expansive critique (Avis, 2007; Jones, 2009; Langemeyer and Roth, 2006; Warmington, 2008). The primary objections have focused on two problems in the ontology of the approach. First, critics have argued that CHAT misunderstands and de-historicizes Marx's theorization of capitalism by introducing the concept of activity. By articulating 'activity' as the 'germ cell' of social analysis, as opposed to Marx's germ cell of the commodity, CHAT theorists have erased both social relations and history from their under-standing of human activity. Activity as 'species character', within the CHAT framework, is disconnected from modes of production and focuses only on human activity as simply activity, and thus as ahistorical activity. The second critique has argued that, given CHAT's starting point in activity, the framework misunderstands the fundamental contradictions of capitalism. This critique positions CHAT as unable to meet its own claims, particularly concerning critical learning and consciousness in workplaces, because it does not understand central contradictions within the formulation of labour power in capitalism, including use value–exchange value and labour–capital. CHAT is only able to address peripheral contradictions and is thus reformist in its tendencies. Further, CHAT's arguments concerning alienation do not draw on a robust understanding of labour power, and thus re-inscribe fragmentation rather than overcome it.

Colley (2010) introduced a deeply important element of this critique by offering a feminist analysis using Marx's analytical tools of essence and appearance. Colley argues that the ahistorical construction of activity within CHAT is actually an abstraction in which activity as a 'species character' is understood as absolute and thus is only able to engage with the appearance of activity. Activity is, she argues, never abstract or neutral; it can only be understood as human labour transformed through capitalism into a kind of 'unfree' activity sold on the commodity market as labour power and so exploited. Within this process labour becomes not just 'human activity' in contradiction with capital, but becomes capital itself. This essential, dialectical contradiction cannot be seen. Colley's critique is developed in the context of her work on emotional labour performed within the politics of care in public services (2012). Further, Colley (2015) argues that there can be no form of labour or activity that is not gendered or racialized within the relations of patriarchal, racist capitalism and thus CHAT begins with assumptions that do not allow the complexity of social relations to become visible. Finally, in her response to other critiques of CHAT, Colley reiterates that its problems lie not in the type of data it produces, but in the ontology and epistemology embodied within. She redirects our attention to the lived experience of women workers and positions their standpoint as the entry point of research.

Given some of the challenges present in researching consciousness, let alone its 'critical' forms, we argue that it is essential to embrace a feminist historical materialist epistemology and ontology for research. Dorothy E. Smith has best formulated the extension of this foundation into an approach for research through her articulation of institutional ethnography. In what follows we discuss our reading of this approach, and continue this elaboration in Chapter 7 with our research in democracy promotion activities in the context of neoliberalism and imperialism.

The philosophical base of institutional ethnography

According to Smith (1990), traditional forms of inquiry in the social sciences begin in what Marx and Engels (1968) called 'the hegemony of the spirit', meaning that these forms of inquiry begin with fundamentally idealist assumptions. Idealist ontology, which even today can be situated within the positivist anxiety of the social sciences, is the belief that social reality is brought into being through human consciousness. This perspective 'never manages to conceive the sensuous world as the total living sensuous activity of the individuals composing it' (Marx and Engels, 1968, p. 42). Social reality remains in the realm of ideas as the driving force of history, rather than, as Marx and Engels propose, the material activity of individuals participating in social relations and co-operation.

It is difficult to make sense of a social reality that is presumed to exist only in the minds of people, a social reality ossified into conceptual categories such as 'structures' and 'systems'. In *The German Ideology*, Marx and Engels detail these processes, and Smith (1990) adopts their analysis in her critique of sociology. For Smith, idealist inquiry begins when the researcher identifies an actual phenomenon in the social world. The researcher collects data on this topic, usually by studying individuals. This 'data' is then taken as evidence apart from the conditions under which it was generated. This happens by using a pre-conceived interpretative framework to make sense of the data. The data is then arranged to make sense in the context of the framework. Marx and Engels referred to this process as making 'mystical connections'. Finally, the resulting arrangement is translated into a concept, which in turn is given the ability to direct relationships between other concepts, such as causality or correlation. As we discussed in Chapter 1, this method of reasoning was identified by Marx and Engels as ideological in the sense that it relies on abstractions from social reality to generate its claims. This sense of ideology is quite different from the sense of ideology as an oppressive system of ideas (Allman, 1999, 2001; Smith 1990). Ideology here is understood in its negative sense, as an epistemology based on the abstraction of experience and knowledge from material and social conditions; it is negative not in the sense that it is 'bad', but as an active negation of the material as actual human practice and forms of consciousness – the negation of praxis.

Ideological reasoning and idealist ontology result in the generation of theoretical concepts and frameworks. Theories and concepts 'as such are not ideological. They are ideological by virtue of being distinctive methods of reasoning and interpreting society' (Smith, 1990, p. 36). This is not to say that categories and concepts do not become laden with relations of power. Nevertheless, Marx and Engels were puzzled as to how these concepts hold such sway. Ideological categories, despite processes of abstraction and mystification, have resonance with actual experience. As such they are important. Smith describes categories in this way:

> Concepts, ideology, and ideological practices are integral parts of socio-historical processes. Through them people grasp in abstraction the real relations of their own lives. Yet while they express and reflect actual social relations, ideological practices render invisible the actualities of people's activities in which those relations arise and by which they are ordered. (1990, pp. 36–7)

The problem with these categories is that they leave undisturbed the ground upon which they are built. The social relations that give rise to certain experiences are not the subject of inquiry; instead, inquiry is confined to the manipulation of concepts and speculation. The result is the entrenchment of the interpretive domain in social inquiry, a fetishized concept of experience, torn apart from its inherently social character and driven by hidden theories. Theory, not experience, is used to make sense of the world, and our sense of the social world as a historical project with real social relations is lost.

This process is extremely problematic. On one level there is the simple issue of perpetuating ideological understandings of the world and the unequal social relations they naturalize and obscure. For Smith, this is an obstruction of inquiry. There is also the problem of objectification. One of the central questions driving Marx was the issue of how it is that human relations come to be used 'over and against' individuals. How it is that something that is merely organized human relations becomes understood as a 'structure' or 'system' that dominates and dictates human experience. The experience of objectified social relations is a result of ideological reasoning. Of equal concern to Smith are the results of these practices on epistemology, particularly as it relates to the experience of women. The alienation of experience and material reality present in traditional forms of social inquiry serve to subjugate women's experience in the world by erasing their materiality from what is known. The result is a sociology that explains away the experiences of women rather than accounting for their actual realities within social relations. Thus, ideological distortions, in the epistemological sense, become ideological distortions in the sense of power.

The ontology of institutional ethnography

As an alternative to these processes, Smith (1990, 2005) argued that social inquiry should begin with the ontology explicated by Marx and Engels in *The German Ideology*. Marx and Engels propose that social inquiry should begin in the real, material processes of life, meaning that inquiry should be directed at actual individuals and their actual experiences and practices. Thus 'the social' is known not as 'society' but through concepts that explain how people actually work and relate as well as how consciousness is formed through this social activity and acts to change human practice. Therefore, ideas, theories and categories arise not only through abstraction, but also through rigorous analysis of human social relations and the material world (Allman, 1999). The individual and the social are dialectically related, meaning that individual action and consciousness have an inner connection with the social totality.

This ontology is taken up through the project of institutional ethnography. Our argument is that separating the social/institutional organization of relationships from actually embodied conscious-ness results in a misreading of institutional ethnography (see Wright and Rocco, 2007). The problem faced by Smith is the question of how to actualize inquiry into this conception of the social. Given our entrenchment in the abstractions and mystifications of traditional forms of inquiry, how do we go about revealing the ideological distortions in our thought and understanding the social relations in which we are bound up? Smith's answer is to begin by making 'the ontological shift'. This shift requires the researcher to work from a definite understanding of the social, which Smith has defined as individuals plus their doings plus co-ordination (Smith, 2007). Working from this definition, based in Marx's ontology, inquiry must always begin with individuals and their actual experiences and practice in relation to others. In making this shift, we move away from understanding the social world as a collection of concepts divorced from people's everyday experience. In order to do this, researchers must begin with the everyday; they must begin with a question as a point of entry and it must be something that the researchers care about. This point of entry is referred to in institu-tional ethnography as the problematic. The problematic must be created from a standpoint (see Chapter 3), which 'creates a point of entry into discovering the social that does not subordinate the knowing subject to objectified forms of knowledge of society or political economy' (Smith, 2005, p. 10). Standpoint serves as a tool to keep the researcher oriented to the subjective position of experience and the real material and social conditions through which subjects experience and make sense of the world. It is only from this embodied subject position that the 'relations of ruling' become visible (Smith, 1997); we examine this concept in the following section. Standpoint, however, is not a phenomenological condition. Other theoretical inscriptions of the embodied subject can lead the researcher away from the actual experiences of the individual in their social world and towards a priori theoretical frameworks. In contrast, Smith argued, standpoint

commits us to beginning in the local historical actualities of one's experience. From this site we can see theories, concepts, and so on, as themselves in and of people's activities, indeed as themselves practices that people bring into play in the ongoing organization of subjectivities that is integral to coordinating activities. (1997, p. 129)

From this perspective experience is understood as disjunctive social relations (Smith, 1988) and as 'the crucible in which the self and the social world enter into a concrete union called "social" subjectivity' (Bannerji, 1995, p. 86). The feminist orientation of standpoint theory, when utilized in an explicitly Marxist framework, allows adult educators to see that human agency and consciousness are integral components of the social organization of social relations (Gorman and Mojab, 2008).

Ruling relations, discourses and texts in institutional ethnography

It is important to remember that the historical condition of Marxist ontology is the understanding that social relations and social reality are not necessarily of one's own making, but take place under conditions of historical necessity (Marx, 1979). Individuals work within historical processes, inheriting material and social relations from the past. Thus, individuals must constantly contend with history and with the understanding that their thinking and being take place within a larger mode of social relations. Using the language of Smith's (2007) definition of the social, there is some social mechanism through which human relations are co-ordinated and organized. This mechanism, however, is not an 'out there' entity such as a structure, but, like capitalism, is itself a process and a relation. Here Smith builds on Marx and identifies this 'something' as ruling relations (1999, 2005).

The notion of ruling relations is the subject of much confusion among students of institutional ethnography. Given the emphasis on institutions and texts, the ruling relations are sometimes mistaken for bureaucracy, individuals, or even the texts themselves. Ruling relations are not things, systems, or people, nor is it a concept equivalent to domination or hegemony. The concept of ruling relations runs contrary to a structural ontology that sees power as somehow outside of social relations. Given Smith's emphasis on Marxist ontology, the ruling relations are a 'complex of objectified social relations that organize and regulate our lives in contemporary society' (Smith, 1999, p. 73). Smith (2007) also refers to 'the ruling relations' as 'the relations that rule' or 'relations of ruling' in order to dispel an interpretation of them as a top-down hegemonic exercising of power or of structures external to human social organization. Ruling relations are 'forms of consciousness and organization that are objectified in the sense that they are constituted externally to particular people or places' (Smith, 2005, p. 13). They are collaborative social relations and forms of consciousness that have taken on the character of existing both inside and outside individuals; they are relations that arise through ideological mechanisms.

Within institutional ethnography, the concept of the ruling relations is very closely tied to the notion of discourse. The term discourse is a loaded term in the social sciences and we will say from the beginning that Smith's conception of discourse is quite different from other usages. Discourse, for Smith (2007), stems from looking at the way social relations, individual actions and consciousness are organized in a particular way. More popular notions of discourse, typically following Foucault, conceptualize discourse in terms of forms of power embedded in language, in particular acts of speaking, statements and texts (Palmer, 1990). This form of discourse, however, still locates knowledge outside of individuals and their experience, as it constructs particular subjectivities for individuals (Smith, 2005). Smith (1999) discusses this form of discourse as important to the study of ruling relations. From her perspective, Foucauldian discourse analysis explicates a particular dimension of the ruling relations, and it can be seen as a complementary process to textual analysis in institutional ethnography (Smith and Schryer, 2007) as it 'captures the displacement of locally situated subjects' (Smith, 1999, p. 80). However, this form of discourse

> leaves unanalysed the socially organized practices and relations that objectify, even those visible in discourse itself. Its constitutional rules confine subjects to a standpoint in discourse and hence in the ruling relations. They eliminate the matrix of local practices of actual people that brings objectification of discourse into existence. (1999, p. 80)

For institutional ethnographers, discourse refers not just to language, but to the totality of social relations mediated by texts (Smith, 2007). A discourse is not an entity of knowledge existing outside individuals, but a particular arrangement of social relations in which people are active participants. This difference is best explained in Smith's (2005) discussion of institutional discourses. These are discourses embodied in particular institutions or complexes of social relations. An example might be the discourse of teacher–student relationships. This discourse co-ordinates activity within the institutional setting of the school, but it also organizes relations between individuals and knowledge. It is embedded with relations of power and domination, but it is a discourse that teachers, students, parents, administrators, politicians and the general community participate in every day. We enact this discourse and bring it to life; it organizes our consciousness and activity. Discourse can be understood as the particular arrangement of social relations co-ordinated and organized through ruling relations. When institutional ethnographers begin their inquiry with a problematic, they develop this problematic in concert with critical reflection on their own location within a discourse, a location also known as standpoint.

It is Smith's (1999, 2005) contention that discourse and ruling relations are observable in talk, texts and institutions. Institutional ethnography maintains a special and dynamic focus on texts as the central mediating body of ruling relations. Ruling relations are conceived of as embedded within texts, whereas the historical development of a text-mediated society brought the ruling relations into existence. Smith (2005) sees textual mediation – including computer technology – as an essential component of the contemporary world. It is her contention that contemporary society has developed into a social reality dependent on texts for communication, organization and regulation, which is to say, the large-scale co-ordination of multiple sites. Historical developments in technologies, particularly print and now computer technologies, allow for the mass replication of texts across time and space, thus instilling in texts a regulatory function across multiple local sites of activity. Texts utilized across multiple sites function in a variety of ways. Some texts create textual communities through which individuals are organized based on a common interpretation and significance attached to text (Smith and Schryer, 2007). Religious bodies associated with core texts (the Bible, the Koran, the Torah) would be examples of these textual communities. Texts also operate through institutions to co-ordinate social relations, thus these processes of textual mediation are the primary focus of institutional ethnography. Texts embedded in institutions almost take on a life of their own. According to Smith, 'the materiality of the text and its replicability create a peculiar ground in which it can seem that language, thought, culture, formal organization, have their own being, outside lived time and the actualities of people's living' (1999, p. 79). This understanding of texts makes clear the relationship between the way texts function in society and the objectified consciousness of the ruling relations.

Smith uses the term 'text' in a broad manner. The term does not just refer to written language, but to other forms of representation, including images, that are replicated and utilized across multiple sites. Smith also rejects post-structuralist theorizing on texts that places them solely within the interpretive realm, in that texts are actual things that exist in an actual space. They are taken up by readers at different times and activated in different ways. Texts exert a regulatory capacity, but they are much more than sets of rules or directives that readers blindly follow. Smith and Schryer argue that:

> Co-ordinating people's doings through the multiplication of identical texts takes for granted that a given text will be interpreted in different local contexts. Texts penetrate and organize the very texture of daily life as well as the always-developing foundations of the social relations and organization of science, industry, commerce, and the public sphere. (2007, p. 116)

In this way, texts function in a similar manner to the ways in which, according to Marx and Engels (1968), abstract conceptualizations help to order consciousness. But they go beyond this function in that they also organize behaviour and co-ordinate action. Ellen Pence's (1997) institutional ethnography on domestic violence demonstrates this dual process. Through her research, Pence shows how texts utilized by police in the course of domestic violence intervention not only shape the consciousness of police on gender-based violence, but also co-ordinate their actual practice of policing these offenses. Texts function as the carriers of institutional discourses, making explicit the ways in which individuals are 'hooked in' to larger social relations through these institutional processes.

Texts, and institutional texts in particular, work as organizers and co-ordinators of social relations. This is the very process described by the concept of ruling relations. Based on Smith's (2005, 2007; Smith and Schryer, 2007) understanding of texts, it is clear that texts are an integral part in the formation of institutional discourses. Institutional discourses are embodied and enacted through texts. However, Smith cautions us not to interpret these relations as ones in which discourses and texts dictate activities. Rather, we should see discourses and texts as 'providing the terms under which what people do becomes institutionally accountable' (2005, p. 113). They frame activities, agents, subjects, behaviours and relations only in institutional terms, using institutional categories. This ideological process again obscures and evacuates individual experience and the 'hooking in' of individuals and institutional processes into social and material relations. In this way, institutional texts and discourses produce regulating discourses. Explication of a given regulating discourse and the mapping of its associated social relations is the ultimate goal of institutional ethnography.

Institutional ethnography as approach, not methodology

Smith (2005) is very clear that institutional ethnography is not a methodology and she goes so far as to assert that it also is not a theory. As we have observed in conference presentations and through discussions of institutional ethnography with a wide variety of researchers, the claim that institutional ethnography is not a theory or a methodology but an approach is the source of much confusion and debate. To be clear on our terms, Smith is using methodology to refer to a way of conducting research that brings with it an already predetermined framework for analysing and interpreting data. Furthermore, we believe she uses the term 'theory' here in its ideological sense, as in theory generated through the abstraction and generalization of experience from social and material relations. This confusion arises because we are: 1) grappling with the positivist legacy that leads us to believe that our research methods are neutral and objective; and 2) we have not fleshed out the entrenchment of ideological modes of reasoning within our approaches to research.

If we understand that institutional ethnography is built on a foundation of Marxist feminist ontology and epistemology – and, as such, is a method of *inquiry* that rejects ideological reasoning, is grounded in historical materialism, and seeks to undo the objectification, masculinization and racialization of the subject – then we will see that institutional ethnography is a process, a method of inquiry, that makes social organization visible, but which does not explain why those social relations exist. Bertell Ollman perhaps said it best when describing Marx's dialectics as a method:

> Dialectics is not a rock-ribbed triad of thesis-antithesis-synthesis that serves as an all-purpose explanation; nor does it provide a formula that enables us to prove or predict anything; nor is it the motor force of history. The dialectic, as such, explains nothing, proves nothing, predicts nothing, and causes nothing to happen. Rather dialectics is a way of thinking that brings into focus the full range of changes and interactions that occur in the world. (1993, p. 10)

Institutional ethnography, of which Marx's dialectical ontology is a core component, behaves in the same fashion. It gives us the tools to see, to actualize, an understanding of the social that otherwise remains hidden under layers of ideology and mystification. In this way it is not an explanatory theory; it is not a framework for interpreting the social. It is a framework for conceptualizing the social. Because of this, we need theory, but we have to be very careful; we do not need theory based on ideology. We need theory generated through the rigorous empirical work of dialectical historical materialism. This is one reason why we advocate for an explicit and vigilant Marxist feminist reading of institutional ethnography.

Institutional ethnography directs research towards social phenomena existing below the surface of appearance. As previously discussed, research in education often struggles with what Smith (2005) described as either the absence of or an overemphasis on the individual. Institutional ethnography offers a way out of this dilemma by situating inquiry within the daily experiences of individuals, their practices and their work while attempting to locate their individual practice within larger institutional discourses and social relations at the same time. This allows us as researchers to see the ways in which discourses and social relations co-ordinate and organize educational and epistemological relations. It allows us to see the ways in which these relationships impact and shape and in turn are shaped by educational practice, particularly in terms of pedagogy and curriculum. It also allows us to see, at the ground level, the pervasiveness and contradictions of ideological reasoning and ideological explanations, particularly in regards to education as a solution for social inequality within liberal capitalist democracies. Most importantly, institutional ethnography provides us with a concrete tool for exploring the intricacies of consciousness and praxis.

Our interest in critical education overlaps with our ongoing examination of liberal democracies, particularly the ways in which states engage in a politics of citizenship and democracy. Our interest in this area focuses on the ways in which states promote particular formations of political subjectivity among their citizenries, how these discourses are enacted through educational programming, towards what ends these formations are directed, and what formation of consciousness results from these social arrangements. Drawing from our own experience conducting research in the field of citizenship education and democracy promotion, institutional ethnography provides windows into the limitations of current lines of inquiry and exposes questions that are otherwise obscured. In our experience, such current lines of inquiry began with a literature review. Literature on citizenship education tends to reflect sets of polemics, with different groups arguing for their own version of the ideal citizen, often by attempting to provide empirical evidence of how these processes are learned. We observed very early on the ways in which this body of literature, while significant in its various contributions to knowledge, does not move beyond an idealist approach to citizenship. Institutional ethnography turns the researcher's attention away from this quagmire and allows an exploration of citizenship as an ideological category and citizenship education as an ideological practice. Our attention is redirected towards the actual social relations that comprise the category of citizenship. We are able to question not just how citizenship education instils certain paradigms of participation or democratic aspirations in learners, but how the concept of citizenship organizes social relations and how that organizational form is supported through educational projects. Institutional ethnography allows us to explore in a deeper way the relationships between citizenship, the state, ideology and democracy. The approach of institutional ethnography moves beyond questions of how one becomes a good citizen to questions of how citizenship education is hooked in to other social relations. Attention is directed away from the abstraction of shaping political subjectivity towards an understanding of how political subjectivity is shaped within existing social relations. Institutional ethnography helps to expose contradictions in ongoing social relations, particularly racialized and gendered class relations.

To summarize, institutional ethnography as an approach to inquiry begins with Marxist ontology and rejects the ideological premises of traditional forms of social inquiry. It conceives of the social as the co-ordination of ongoing human relations and activity. As such, the focus of inquiry is the mechanisms of co-ordination, understood as the ruling relations. An emphasis on the ordering of social relations and the dialectical relationship between social relations, consciousness and material practices is at the centre of the project of institutional ethnography. It is our contention that institutional ethnography offers a compelling path for inquiry in critical education. Institutional ethnography allows educational researchers to move away from individualized notions of learning that not only reinforce ideological reasoning, but support a learning paradigm that colludes with the capitalist project of the entrepreneurial individual and its raced, gendered and classed dimensions (Gorman, 2007). By using institutional ethnography to advance a Marxist feminist understanding of consciousness, we can direct educational research towards the explication of these dimensions and social transformation.

As theorists and practitioners of critical adult education we have long focused our attention on raising or transforming the consciousness of adult learners. We have developed theoretical and pedagogical traditions such as transformative learning and popular education that work to implement this vision. We have given far less serious consideration to how we come to understand the praxis of consciousness itself. We have often lapsed into working from the outside in, with results that many would find less than extraordinary. How can we move forward with a revolutionary educational project if we do not know how to understand consciousness empirically and not just theoretically? We can consider the value of institutional ethnography by returning to the social purposes of critical adult education or perhaps even adult education in general. Recent calls for such a return invite us to adapt new tools and approaches within our field that present us with opportunities to move beyond top-down theorization or practice and away from our asocial indulgence in the self (Martin, 2008). A Marxist feminist reading of institutional ethnography offers the potential to ground educational inquiry in the real experiences of learners in their social complexity, with the possibility of illuminating results.

References

Allman, P. (1999) *Revolutionary social transformation: Democratic hopes, political possibilities and critical education* (Westport, CT: Bergin & Garvey).

— (2001) *Critical education against global capitalism: Karl Marx and revolutionary critical education* (Westport, CT: Bergin & Garvey).

Avis, J. (2007) 'Engeström's version of activity theory: A conservative praxis?', *Journal of Education and Work*, Vol. 20, No. 3, 161–77.

Bannerji, H. (1995) *Thinking through: Essays on feminism, Marxism, and anti-racism* (Toronto: Women's Press).

Cammarota, J. and Fine, M. (eds) (2008) *Revolutionizing education: Youth participatory action research in motion* (New York: Routledge).

Carpenter, S. (2011) *Theorizing praxis in citizenship learning: Civic engagement and the democratic management of inequality in AmeriCorps*, unpublished thesis, Toronto: University of Toronto.

Choudry, A. (2015) *Learning activism: The intellectual life of contemporary social movements* (Toronto: University of Toronto Press).

Colley, H. (2010) 'A rough guide to CHAT from an historical materialist perspective', lecture, OISE/University of Toronto.

— (2012) 'Not learning in the workplace: Austerity and the shattering of *illusion* in public service', *Journal of Workplace Learning*, Vol. 24, No. 5, 317–37.

— (2015) 'Labour power', in S. Mojab (ed.), *Marxism and feminism* (London: Zed), pp. 221–38.

Engeström, Y. (2001) 'Expansive learning at work: Towards an activity theoretical reconceptualization', *Journal of Education and Work*, Vol. 14, No. 1, 133–56.

Foley, G. (1999) *Learning in social action: A contribution to understanding informal education* (London: Zed).

Grahame, K.M. (1998) 'Asian women, job training and the social organization of immigrant labor markets', *Qualitative Sociology*, Vol. 21, No. 1, 75–90.

Gruner, S. (2012) *Learning land and life: An institutional ethnography of land use planning and development in a northern Ontario First Nation*, unpublished thesis, Toronto: University of Toronto.

Gorman, R. (2007) 'The feminist standpoint and the trouble with "informal learning": A way forwards for Marxist-feminist educational research', in A. Green, G. Rikowski and H. Raduntz (eds), *Renewing dialogues in Marxism and education: Openings* (New York: Palgrave Macmillan), pp. 183–99.

Gorman, R. and Mojab, S. (2008) 'War, diaspora, learning, and women's standpoint', in M. Hajdukowski-Ahmed, N. Khanlou and H. Moussa (eds), *Not born a refugee woman: Contesting identities, rethinking practices* (New York: Berghahn), pp. 135–49.

Hall, B., Clover, D., Crowther, J. and Scandrett, E. (2011) 'Social movement learning: A contemporary re-examination', *Studies in the Education of Adults*, Vol. 43, No. 2, 113–16.

Holst, J. (2011) 'Frameworks for understanding the politics of social movements', *Studies in the Education of Adults*, Vol. 43, No. 2, 117–27.

Jackson, N. (1995) '"These things just happen": Talk, text, and curricular reform', in M. Campbell and A. Manicom (eds), *Knowledge, experience, and ruling relations* (Toronto: University of Toronto Press), pp. 164–80.

Jones, P. (2009) 'Breaking away from *Capital*? Theorising activity in the shadow of Marx', *Outlines: Critical Practice Studies*, Vol. 11, No. 1, 45–58.

Kapoor, D. and Jordan, S. (eds) (2009) *Education, participatory action research, and social change* (Berlin: Springer).

Langemeyer, I. and Roth, W. (2006) 'Is Cultural Historical Activity Theory threatening to fall short of its own principles and possibilities as a dialectical social science', *Outlines*, Vol. 8, No. 2, 20–42.

McIntyre, A. (2008) *Participatory action research* (London: Sage).

Martin, I. (2008) 'Whither adult education in the learning paradigm? Some personal reflections'. Plenary address to the 38th Annual SCUTREA Conference, 2–4 July 2008, University of Edinburgh. Available at www.scutrea.ac.uk.

Marx, K. (1979 [1852]) *The Eighteenth Brumaire of Louis Bonaparte*, in *Collected Works*, Vol. 11. (Moscow: Progress).

Marx, K. and Engels, F. (1968 [1846]) *The German ideology*, trans. S. Ryazanskaya (Moscow: Progress).

Mezirow, J. (1991) *Transformative dimensions of adult learning* (San Francisco: Jossey-Bass).

— (ed.) (2000) *Learning as transformation* (San Francisco: Jossey-Bass).

Ng, R. (1988) *The politics of community services* (Toronto: Garamond).

— (1995) 'Multiculturalism as ideology: A textual analysis', in M. Campbell and A. Manicom (eds), *Knowledge, experience, and ruling relations* (Toronto: University of Toronto Press), pp. 35–48.

Ollman, B. (1993) *Dialectical investigations* (New York: Routledge).

— (n.d.) *A model of activist research: How to study class consciousness … and why we should*, self-published. Available at www.nyu.edu/projects/ollman/docs/class_consciousness.php.

O'Sullivan, E. (1999) *Transformative learning: Educational vision for the 21st century* (London: Zed).

Palmer, B. (1990) *Descent into discourse: The reification of language and the writing of social history* (Philadelphia: Temple University Press).

Pence, E. (1997) *Safety for battered women in a textually mediated legal system*, unpublished doctoral dissertation, Toronto: University of Toronto.

Sawchuk, P., Duarte, N. and Elhammoumi, M. (eds) (2006) *Critical perspectives on activity: Explorations across education, work, and everyday life* (Cambridge: Cambridge University Press).

Smith, D.E. (1988) *The everyday world as problematic* (Toronto: University of Toronto Press).

— (1990) *The conceptual practices of power: A feminist sociology of knowledge* (Boston: Northeastern University Press).

— (1997) 'From the margins: Women's standpoint as a method of inquiry in the social sciences', *Gender, Technology, and Development*, Vol. 1, No. 1, 113–35.

— (1999) *Writing the social: Critique, theory, and investigations* (Toronto: University of Toronto Press).

— (2005) *Institutional ethnography: A sociology for people* (Lanham: AltaMira Press).

— (2007) Institutional ethnography workshop, delivered 17–19 August at Ontario Institute for Studies in Education at the University of Toronto, Canada.

Smith, D.E. and Schryer, C.F. (2007) 'On documentary society', in C. Bazerman (ed.), *Handbook on research on writing: History, society, school, individual, text* (Mahwah: Lawrence Erlbaum), pp. 113–27.

Warmington, P. (2008) 'From "activity" to "labor": Commodification, labour-power, and contradiction in Engeström's activity theory', *Outlines: Critical Practice Studies*, Vol. 10, No. 2, 4–19.

Wilmot, S. (2011) *The social organization of the Ontario minimum wage campaign*, unpublished thesis, Toronto: University of Toronto.

Wright, U.T., and Rocco, T.S. (2007) 'Institutional ethnography: A tool for interrogating the institutional and political conditions of individual experience', in L. Servage and T. Fenwick (eds), *Joint international conference of AERC and CASAE: 26th National Conference* (Halifax: University of Nova Scotia), pp. 643–48.

6

Capitalist Imperialism as Social Relations: Implications for Praxis, Pedagogy and Resistance

In April 2016 academics, activists and networks of Afro-Colombian and indigenous women in Buenaventura, Colombia organized a forum on 'The Assassination of Women and Global Accumulation' to discuss the rise of political and personal violence against women in the Pacific region of Colombia. The notion of 'femicide' – that is, the killing, disappearing and threatening of women – was at the core of the discussions. The forum was a feminist space of collective deliberation and exchange of experiences of, and resistance to, violence against women, with participants from Africa, the Middle East and the Americas. Stories of multiple forms of violence against women, such as sexual violence, forced prostitution and harassment by military and paramilitary groups were told, in addition to the accounts of femicide. We heard about the violent displacement and destruction of Afro-Colombian and indigenous communities, of targeted assassinations, intimidation, and threats against their leaders and human rights activists. We also learned that 'Colombia experiences the second highest number of femicides after Mexico' (Sanchez-Garzoli, 2012, p. 7). This level of violence is co-ordinated and maintained by the patriarchal, racist and capitalist forces of the Colombian state, by military and paramilitary groups, by narco-traffickers and by the mining operations of giant transnational companies such as Exxon-Mobil, among many others. The women's stories of violence, displacement, racism and dispossession were horrifying; nonetheless, we had to overcome the sense of despair as we observed the determination of so many women, young and old, to make an effort to change their individual and collective conditions.

While there is much to discuss about this important forum, which we intend to do in another space, one contentious issue became the impetus for writing this chapter, namely, the understanding of colonialism and imperialism. The necessity of understanding colonialism and imperialism can be heard across various intellectual and activist spaces, both feminist and non-feminist. Within educational theory, there has been much discussion of the phenomena of colonialism and imperialism as well as of neoliberalism and capitalism, as we have mentioned earlier, particularly in Chapter 1. A lack of conceptual clarity results in what we call the 'buzz words' phenomenon amongst our graduate students – bare life, the commons and decolonizing are all used without a clear understanding of their content or purpose, and with a reliance on eclectic, and sometimes paradoxical, use of theory. We very much want, as adult educators, to respond to the conditions we see in our material world and to problems that educators must think through as they relate to learning and revolution, but as we have reiterated throughout this book, this requires critical interrogation of our use of concepts.

At the forum, violence against women was mostly and correctly associated with the displacement and dispossession of Afro-Colombian and indigenous communities. Historical moments of colonization were recalled. While the ghost of colonialism was haunting us, it was difficult to pin it down. As capitalism, old and new, was imposingly present in the discussions, in the conference rooms, and in the streets and landscape of Buenaventura, our understanding was constrained by current theoretical and political tendencies to delink capitalism and imperialism, tendencies that declare the end of imperialism and that present the world as one of 'post-coloniality' and 'empire'. Some rejected the concept of imperialism as being a relic of the left movements; quite often, when the concepts of colonialism and imperialism were used, they were treated as interchangeable and so synonymous; others considered the occupation of land and the brutal displacement of communities to be the continuation of colonization. Some treated the use of financial markets to control local economics as forms of neo-colonialism. Conceptualizations such as anti-colonialism, anti-imperialism, or national liberation movements were forgotten in debates about the Global South. Thus, we began to wonder if consciousness about capitalist imperialism as *social relations*, connecting peoples and communities through a myriad of complex and contradictory relations, lags behind its omnipresence throughout the world. Therefore, in this chapter we begin with a brief historical sketch of the concepts of imperialism and colonialism before considering contemporary theoretical and political debates and discussing their extension into the realm of culture, ideology and pedagogy in order to think through the places and spaces of anti-imperialist resistance.

Capitalism is changing our planet more aggressively than any previous mode of production. We now know more about the racialized and gendered nature of the formation of capitalism and its subsequent transformation into imperialism. The changing nature of labour, capital, financialization, (re)production and technology, as well as social relations within capitalism, has invited much research and theorization. Education has been indispensable to capitalism to the extent that critical education, as we have extensively discussed in this book and elsewhere, fails to be critical if it is not based on a dialectical and historical under-standing of the conflicted relationship between consciousness, learning, ideology and capitalist imperialism (Mojab, 2011). We do not intend to repeat those analyses here; instead, this chapter highlights trends in the development of capitalism, colonialism, imperialism and some of the key debates on the topic.

Colonialism and imperialism: history/theory

Imperialism is not principally a military project – despite the significance of force to the way it operates – and to conceive of it in this way is to mistake the outward appearances of Western intervention for its essence. Rather, imperialism is primarily about ensuring the ongoing subordination of the region's political economy to the forms of accumulation in the core capitalist states of the world market. Seen in this light, neoliberalism is much more than simply a menu of 'free market' economic policies: it represents a radical restructuring of class relations that acts to facilitate and reinforce the region's domination by external powers. In so doing, it generates a set of social forces that are internal to the region itself, and that have an objective stake in supporting the new status quo. This restructuring has not just involved the transformation of class and state within individual nation-states but has also produced a new set of hierarchies and intermeshing of social relations across the regional space as a whole. (Hanieh, 2013, p. 46)

Following Hanieh's analysis, we understand imperialism in terms of social relations, class relations and class struggle, and as having a complex and dynamic relation to colonialism. The term 'imperialism', according to the *Oxford English Dictionary* (OED), was first used in 1878 to indicate 'the advocacy of holding political dominion or control over dependent countries', although its first usage as 'an imperial system of government' dates back to 1684 (OED, 2014). The OED states that 'colonialism' in the sense of 'the colonial system or principle' (OED, 1891a) appeared also in the latter part of the nineteenth century, but the adjective 'colonial' with the meaning 'of, belonging to, or relating to a colony', referring specifically to the British colonies, was in use a century earlier (OED, 1891b). While the two competing terms continue to occupy the same semantic space, their theoretical and lived experiences are significantly different. The terms have had different trajectories although they are both often used to explain the expansion of capitalism from the sixteenth through to the nineteenth centuries. More recently, some sources have called the era of European colonialism (sixteenth century to the late nineteenth century) 'old imperialism' and that of 1870 to 1914 'new imperialism'; the latter period has also been called the 'Age of Imperialism' (Saccarelli and Varadarajan, 2015).

Wood (2003) has argued that the concept of 'colonialism' specifies the conquest of territories and the appropriation of their natural and human resources. Further, and this is key to the present discussion, she argued that concepts such as 'colony' cannot be used in a trans-historical sense nor can the concept of 'empire' be conflated with 'imperialism'. While peripheral territories have long been a component of the building of empires, including non-capitalist empires, the English term 'colonialism' acquired administrative, legal and political significance with the rise of capitalism in sixteenth-century Europe, when a number of countries such as Portugal, Spain, the Netherlands, Italy and later England and France colonized extensive territories in Asia, Africa and the Americas. Thus the term 'colonialism' should be used with this historical specificity in mind. The British government created the position of Secretary of State for the Colonies in 1768, a position only abolished in 1966, while the term 'colony' remained in official use until 1981 (Wood, 2003). The term 'colony' and its derivatives were also used in the widespread resistance movements against colonial rule, as in anti-colonialism, decolonization, neo-colonialism, and more recently post-colonialism.

While territorial expansionism was the actual policy of both colonialism and imperialism, some intellectuals and activists on the left were not satisfied with the simplistic equation of imperialism and expansionism. Radical changes in European and North American capitalisms, beginning in the latter part of the nineteenth century in the wake of the Second Industrial Revolution, required more adequate theories of imperialism. This development, involving the transition from mercantile, free competition to monopoly capitalism, was labelled as 'imperialism' by, among others, John Hobson (1902), Rosa Luxemburg (1951) and Rudolph Hilferding (1981), and was adopted as a concept by Lenin in his influential work, *Imperialism: The Highest Stage of Capitalism* (1967).

This late nineteenth and early twentieth-century period of world history is popularly understood and remembered through such images as the robber baron industrialist and the anti-monopoly crusades of the progressive reform era. The transformation into monopolies was made possible by both the nature of capital (in popular parlance, 'expand or die') and industrial production; it included the emergence of financial capital and a new round of international rivalries for securing territories and 'spheres of influence' through colonial wars and agreements for re-dividing the world. These developments gave rise to new debates among liberals and conservatives on the one hand, and opponents of capitalism such as anarchists, communists and socialists on the other, over how to understand militarism, nationalism and internationalism. These disputes did not lead to theoretical precision in so far as imperialism was largely understood as a state policy that could be adopted or discarded at will rather than as socioeconomic relations that bound together multiple global geographies.

For the liberal scholar Hobson (1902), imperialism was a policy rooted in the immoral and disproportionate distribution of wealth in capitalism, a wrong that could be corrected. This position reflects, exclusively, an engagement with the *appearance* of imperialism, that is, with the conditions of war and growing inequality. For Lenin (1967), by contrast, imperialism was the highest stage in capitalism, which necessitated a call for the internationalism of the working class and the rejection of *nationalist*-based anti-war movements. Imperialism, in this theorization, is capitalism distinguished from its earlier mercantile stage by the following features: 1) the continuing concentration of production and capital, which leads to the creation of monopolies dominating the economy; as such imperialism is monopoly capitalism, the opposite of free competition capitalism; 2) bank capital and industrial capital merge to form finance capital and a huge financial oligarchy; 3) the export of capital takes precedence over the export of commodities; 4) imperialist powers struggle to secure spheres of influence, colonies and semi-colonies; and 5) the territorial division of the world among the monopolies leads to fierce competition for the re-division of the world, usually through war.

This theorization was not a simple amending of the Marxist understanding of capitalism or a spicing up of Hobson's idea of imperialism. In fact, the transition from free competition to monopoly capitalism entailed theorizing not only a new stage of capitalism but also a new stage in class struggle. During the lifetime of Marx, revolution was thought to be possible only in the developed capitalist countries, involving the two major and antagonistic classes of the bourgeoisie and the proletariat. Lenin argued that imperialism, having intensified all the contradictions of capitalism on an international scale, had brought the non-capitalist world into the orbit of the struggle for democracy and self-determination. Imperialism had, in other words, inaugurated 'the era of proletarian social revolution' not only in advanced capitalist societies but also in Asia, Africa and Latin America (Lenin, 1967, p. 678). Carefully observing the advent of bourgeois democratic revolutions on the three continents, and inspired by the two major revolutions in Persia (Iran) in 1906–11 and China in 1911, he declared that the proletariat in Europe, in its struggle against capitalism, had found allies in the colonized world. In an article from 1913 entitled 'Backward Europe and Advanced Asia', he wrote that Europe, 'with its highly developed machine industry, its rich, multiform culture and its constitutions ... supports everything backward, moribund, and medieval'; by contrast, 'everywhere in Asia, a mighty democratic movement is growing, spreading and gaining in strength' (Lenin, 1962, p. 82). This understanding had a profound impact on the politics and programmes of communist parties (known as 'social-democratic parties' before 1917).

The concept of imperialism occupied a hegemonic place in left discourses during the First World War and after the first socialist revolution in Russia in 1917, in the theory and practice of the third Communist International (1919–43), and among anarchist, socialist, communist and national liberation movements. In the early twenty-first century, the concept of imperialism is now being used again as an indispensable aid in explaining the post-Cold War international order marked by the unending wars of the Western powers in the Middle East and Africa, the ongoing economic crises in Europe, North America and the rest of the world, the domination of finance capital, and the continuing rivalry among blocs of capitalist powers both old and new (Wood, 2003; Saccarelli and Varadarajan, 2015). As the imperialist order incessantly changes, the understanding of this order also continues to be the site of theoretical and political struggles, as we discuss below.

Imperialism is not Empire

A major point of contention in debates on imperialism concerns its nature – is it a policy or is it a stage in the development of capitalism? Among the early advocates of imperialism as policy were John Hobson and Karl Kautsky. The latter, for instance, argued that imperialism had eased rather than intensified the contradictions of capital, and the rise of monopolies allowed for 'ultra-imperialism', a global order in which capital peacefully divides the world without the need for world wars. In sharp contrast, Lenin insisted that the rise of imperialism was 'the development and direct continuation of the fundamental characteristics of capitalism in general' (1967, p. 744).

While imperialism brought the pre-capitalist territories of Asia, Africa and Latin America into world capitalist relations, it cannot be reduced to expansionism. It is, more significantly, a process of capitalist accumulation, one which is neither the simple sum of its parts nor a pure expansion in space, but rather a complex network of relations with its own dynamics. It is the intensification of the fundamental contradiction of capitalism between the socialization of production and its private appropriation on an international scale. Imperialism has engaged the majority of the world's population in a colossal division and exchange of labour. The incessant socialization of production and privatization of ownership, a situation highlighted more recently in the slogan of the Occupy Movement's 'We are the 99%', has turned private ownership into an obstacle to the survival of the majority and has seriously endangered the planet's environment. From the point of view of Marxism, this contradiction between private ownership and socialized production can be solved only through the negation of the former and the advancement of the latter into communism. Such a revolution does not, of course, happen spontaneously. This has profound implications for any theorization of critical education or critical forms of consciousness and, thus, conceptual specificity is needed.

In their influential work *Empire* (2000), Hardt and Negri argued that capitalism has changed to the extent that the transition to communism is inevitable and will come about spontaneously. They contend that capitalism has entered a new phase, one that cannot be explained by the Leninist theory of imperialism. This shift happened on the basis of what they call 'immaterial labour', the end of exchange value, the dissolution of private property, the shift from production of material goods to services, and the rise of a 'virtual economy'. In this new epoch they call Empire, the power of the nation-state has declined and capitalism has spread to every quarter of the world, linked by communication and production in entirely new ways, with new forms of labour creating new class formations. They argue that imperialism has been surpassed by a new globalizing system they call Empire, which facilitates the rise of a self-organizing and self-administering humanity. In this era, sovereignty is de-territorialized, leaving room for an increasing mobility of labour, a fluidity of capital, an ongoing migration, and an organizing on an international level allowing human beings to realize the dream of building a world without pillage and piracy and moving towards equality and justice. Theoretically, Hardt and Negri have concluded that 'dialectics is finished and reform (as "refusal of work") is the new name of revolution because, it is assumed, in the new capitalism there is no longer any conflict "between reform and revolution"' (Ebert and Zavarzadeh, 2014, p. 397).

While Hardt and Negri have highlighted significant trends of change in contemporary capitalism, their claims about empire have been challenged both theoretically and empirically. Theoretically, for instance, critics have argued that the law of value continues to govern capitalism in spite of changes in production (Harvey, 2003; McNally, 2009). Also, Federici (2012) has argued that Hardt and Negri's theory is unable to address the social organization of productive and reproductive labour underpinning society. Contrary to Hardt and Negri, other critics argue that borders and state power are reinforced rather than eroded, and the capitalist state impedes the formation of communist society through either reform or spontaneous changes (Ebert and Zavarzadeh, 2014; A.J.K., 2006). The theoretical validity of *Empire* (2000), and a second text *Multitude* (2004), however, has been undermined by the course of events thus far in the twenty-first century, including the economic crisis of 2008, the US-led 'War on Terror' in Afghanistan (2001) and Iraq (2003), the European Union and NATO's war against Libya (2011), the wars in Ukraine, Yemen and Syria, massive poverty, unemployment, uprooting of populations, and waves of refugees and migrants.

Hardt and Negri's theorization of empire converges with the late twentieth-century post-structuralist turn in theory. It is in line with, for instance, Edward Said's stance against determinism and universalism, and his commitment to finding a new, non-centred subject of history, the multitude, instead of the proletariat in Marxist theory (Saccarelli and Varadarajan, 2015). While Hardt and Negri's empire is a historical notion, Said delinked imperialism from capitalism and by doing so arrived at a trans-historical and a-historical understanding, for instance defining imperialism as 'the practice, theory, and attitudes of a dominating metropolitan centre ruling a distant territory' (Said, 1993, p. 8; for a similar critique see Ahmad, 1994). This definition obscures the distinctions between, for example, the forms of imperialism of Portugal, Britain, Canada, the Netherlands and the United States. Imperialism and colonialism are also reduced to cultural and intellectual relationships between metropolitan centres and colonized territories, emphasizing these relationships on the terrain of knowledge and power to the detriment of material social relations.

The centrality of expansion and domination in the conventional, lexical meaning of imperialism allows for the use of the term in combinations like 'cultural imperialism', 'linguistic imperialism', 'media imperialism', 'academic imperialism', 'social imperialism', or 'food imperialism'. Thus, any extension of power beyond a centre is usually conceptualized as a form of imperialism. In Marxist theory, however, imperialism is primarily the development of capitalism in the centre (concentration of production, monopolization, or rise of finance capital), which reshapes both the internal contradictions of socioeconomic relations and the relationships with spheres of influence. To elaborate this point, let us look more closely at the relationship between imperialism and culture with particular reference to the post-9/11 period.

Imperialism, ideology and culture

The current contradiction between imperialism and religious extremisms or fundamentalisms has had a profound impact on race, class and gender relations. The complex interplay between imperialism and fundamental-ism is presented to us as an opposition of forces, for example as a 'clash of civilizations'. However, we argue that while they *appear* to be in conflict, in *essence* they remain on the same side in so far as they are in fact aligned against the eradication of racism, the emancipation of women, and the realization of democracy, freedom, equality, justice, secularism and socialism. In other words, imperialisms and fundamentalisms co-exist and mutually benefit from this co-existence. Much of capitalist imperialism coheres, coincides, colludes and correlates with Christianity, Islam, Judaism, Hinduism, or other forms of religious, cultural or racial extremisms. Let us put it differently. The two forces of imperialism and fundamentalism *reinforce* each other while *opposing* each other; thus, if we support either one, we end up strengthening both. This means that, for instance, the reduction of the war in the Middle East and North African regions or the global project of the War on Terror to the question of either 'fundamentalism' or 'imperialism' distorts the class nature of the struggles. This either/or position strengthens and reinforces funda-mentalism and imperialism. Most significantly though, this distortion turns our attention away from the profound inequalities and oppressive relations that exist within different societies and cultures and also on the world scale, and it promotes instead nationalism and claims to cultural identities. Imperialist powers benefit from the simplistic construction of an enemy, which can be used to mobilize their citizens in support of their own domination. Fundamentalists of diverse tendencies also benefit from promoting nationalism, religion, culture or race as the only source of resistance against imperialist oppression and domination.

Imperialism and its predecessor, colonialism, could not maintain their centuries-long rule solely by means of coercion and military violence, since every act of occupation and domination met with resistance and quite often attracted the support of anti-imperialist forces in metropolitan countries. In their conquest of the Western hemisphere and parts of Africa and Asia, European colonialists, in the form of both the state and commercial powers, resorted to war, and did not hesitate to engage in massacres, ethnic cleansing and genocide (Coulthard, 2014; Linebaugh and Rediker, 2000; Mann, 2004; Smith 2015). Many indigenous populations were labelled 'savages' who could only be either eliminated or civilized and Christianized. In the capitalist centres, eugenics was employed to bring about the hoped-for eventual disappearance of 'inferior races' and indigenous peoples as well as what Fanon (1961) called 'unfit' groups and individuals within the White race. With the rise of imperialism, the ideological and cultural landscape became more complicated due to the spread of mass literacy, mass media, education, political organizing and parliamentary regimes – a situation that demanded a more subtle rationalization for domination. Equally important was the need of the imperialist powers to thwart solidarity between the working classes and advocates of freedom in the metropolitan centres on the one hand, and national liberation and socialist movements in countries under domination on the other.

What Edward Said (1994) has called Orientalism was one major ideological component of colonial rule. Orientalist thought, constructed and propagated in scientific, scholarly, literary, artistic and intellectual works, artificially divided the world into the West and the East, the Occident and the Orient, the familiar and the exotic, the civilized and uncivilized, 'us' and 'them'. The peoples of the East were thus constructed as fully different from and inferior to those of the West, a situation that obliged the standard-bearers of civilization, the White race, to rule over them, rescue them from ignorance, and civilize them. These myths came into full swing in the eighteenth century, and the separation of the East and the West forms, up to the present, a kernel of a colonialist, imperialist, nationalist, religious and nativist ethos. The contemporary discourse post 9/11 is similar to that of earlier nationalist cultures and politics in so far as it is informed by theoretical claims of identity politics, cultural relativism and nativism, which delink capitalism and imperialism, reject internationalism as a grand narrative, and reduce resistance to the realm of culture.

Resistance against imperialism

We may ask, however, what culture is when it is separated from history and social relations. A learning that isolates culture from its material and historical roots is 'a form of liberalism where pluralism is valued above all, and individual conceptions of empowerment are all that matter' (Silver, 2011, p. 204). The individuation and localization of learning in pedagogical terms is reductionist and theoretically is ideological in so far as it impedes the possibility of initiating a process of conscious *becoming* on the part of learners as revolutionary subjects. Our point is that to comprehend the totality of capitalist imperialism, we need to understand that it is an objective reality that exists independently of any individual or geographical location and expresses its complexity in all spheres of life, such as politics, ideology, patriarchy, racism, art, education, culture or religion.

Resistance to colonialism, particularly settler colonialism, has been ongoing for more than 500 years. However, by the end of the nineteenth century the world was under the rule of a dozen imperialist powers. They waged war not only against the colonized peoples, but also against each other. Two new political movements threatened this world order: nationalism in the colonies and socialism in the capitalist world. In many parts of the world, the rise of nationalism shaped these resistance movements into the form of organized, often party-led, struggles for self-determination. Feeling threatened by these movements, imperialist powers such as Britain, France and the United States appealed to tribal, feudal and religious groups against nationalist movements (Khalidi, 2004; Yaqub, 2004).

Within the capitalist countries, the rise of the working class and their unions and political parties heralded a serious challenge to the system, as was experienced in the short-lived history of the Paris Commune in 1871. The main crack in the imperialist order came in 1917 when the world's largest empire, Russia, underwent a socialist revolution, followed by failed revolutions in Germany, Hungary and Italy. The second imperialist war in 1939–45 led to more revolutions and national liberation struggles in, for example, Algeria, China, Cuba, Indonesia, Korea and Vietnam, which further weakened the capitalist front. By the mid twentieth century, the world had been divided into the 'two camps', one of capitalism and socialism, and another of national liberation struggles in Indochina, Africa, Latin America and the Middle East, which constituted a major threat to imperialism. In Vietnam, the 'peasant army' led by communists defeated the French army (in 1954), which in turn inspired, among other struggles, the advent of the Algerian War of Independence (1954–62). The United States, believing that the two old colonial powers, the United Kingdom and France, were unable to protect the 'Free World', asserted its hegemony over the imperialist bloc and launched a total 'war against communism'. The target was not only communist movements and socialist countries, but also national liberation movements and all social movements for justice. This project consisted of regime changes through coups d'état, but also local and proxy wars, occupations, networks of military bases, the building up of the military and intelligence, the establishment of dictatorial regimes, military alliances and aid, a space race and genocide. The Cold War component of this conflict was equally elaborate and included networks of propaganda, the use of religion against the secularism of nationalist and socialist movements, psychological warfare, espionage, and political and ideological control in popular culture, print and broadcast media, film, literature and education (Dreyfus, 2005; Curtis, 2015; Johnson, 2010).

The imperialist order saw significant changes in the latter part of the twentieth century. The national liberation struggles of the 1950s and 1960s led to the independence of many colonies, although political sovereignty did not avert economic and cultural dependence. In imperialist countries, a wave of social movements in the 1960s challenged imperialist and militarist aggression. In the mid twentieth century, struggles such as the US Civil Rights movement, the Algerian war for independence, the Cuban revolution, the Cultural Revolution in China, and the US war against Vietnam contributed to the radicalization of social movements on an international scale. However, in the late twentieth century the struggle against imperialism experienced a major reversal. Capitalism was restored in China in the course of a coup d'état in 1976 (Hinton, 1990); the disintegration of the Soviet bloc, not due to revolutionary anti-imperialism, brought Eastern European countries into the Western bloc and left Russia in the opposite pole. While the United States continues to be the dominant military and economic power, its decline in a rapidly changing multi-polar imperialist order is evident. It would be difficult to deny that Russia, China and India, as well as other emerging powers, display the characteristics of imperialism such as the predominance of financial capital, the existence of monopolies in a variety of new forms, the export of capital, fierce competition over spheres of influence, war and militarization.

All of this is happening in the context of crises in capitalism, often disguised through concepts such as 'globalization', that is, the trend towards integration and interaction among nationally divided capital, labour, production, markets, technology and culture. Since the mid twentieth century, capital–labour relations have changed dramatically; expanding socialization of production has led to the creation of the largest global proletariat ever in the South. In 2010, '79 per cent, or

541 million, of the world's industrial workers lived in "less developed regions". This is up from 34 per cent in 1950 and 53 per cent in 1980' (Smith, 2015, p. 85). While receiving starvation wages well below the value of their labour power, what they produce at very low cost is sold at higher prices in the North, allowing for super profits and the rise of new monopolies. 'Globalization' happens in the midst of rivalries and a scramble for hegemony by blocs of imperialist powers.

In the twentieth century, the contention between imperialist powers unleashed two world wars, fascism, and new re-divisions of the world. In the early twenty-first century, while the dispute among the major powers is building up, a new conflict between imperialism and fundamentalisms has intensified. The primary target of the two sides is the control of the human and natural resources in Muslim majority countries, where they have subjected war-torn populations to brutal repression, leading to large displacements of people in countries such as Iraq, Syria, Libya, Afghanistan and Yemen. This displacement and dispossession includes the unprecedented destruction of villages, cities, and even archaeological monuments, as well as the brutal repression of women and religious and ethnic minorities. The contradiction between labour and capital has also intensified in both the West and new imperialist states such as China and India. While theocratic Islam in the Middle East and North Africa is engaged in enslaving women and religious and ethnic minorities, and brutalizing any source of opposition, capitalist imperialism generates various forms of slavery, bonded labour, sex work, child labour, trafficking of children and women, and the displacement of millions due to wars and human-made disasters. In this context,

We should expect that the polarization of the rich and poor, especially the very rich and the very poor, will widen. In addition, there will be growing tensions between nations and regions over the earth's resources, in particular, fuel, water, and arable land. There also will be further resistance to immigration, and rampant racism will be used to both fuel and rationalize the resistance ... In fact, we can expect the intensification of every conceivable oppression – gender, race, disability, sexuality, ethnicity, and so on – as groups are pitted against one another in the struggle for survival. (Allman, 2010, p. 239)

While poverty and hunger in the midst of enormous wealth character-
izes the dynamics of imperialism (Hedges, 2015; Machin, 2008; Sassen,
2014; Smith, 2016; Whitehead, 2015), worldwide resistance on the part
of workers, peasants, women, slaves, the urban poor, indigenous peoples,
the homeless, the unemployed, environmentalists and others highlights
the significance of the contradiction between imperialism and peoples of
the world. This contradiction is likely to result in revolutions, although
the absence of revolutionary consciousness and praxis will not allow
these spontaneous and disconnected struggles to put an end to the
imperialist system and bring about an international order that negates
oppression and exploitation (Jazayeri, 2015).

The Buenaventura forum on femicide was a reminder that we live
at a time when the rebellion of women against oppression is spreading
internationally and evolving. It is clear that this rebellion will provide a
big part of the explosive power of the new wave of socialist revolutions.
Our knowledge of the dialectics of consciousness and the materiality of
social relations can help us to develop a revolutionary feminist praxis as
one of the key fronts of class struggle, and it can turn socialist ideology
and its programme into a powerful material force. It is through a deep
theoretical and historical engagement with capitalist imperialism that,
first, we can realize that imperialism is capable of reproducing itself, and
second, that it is constituted, expressed and experienced through other
contradictions, including those of gender, race, sexuality, nationality,
ethnicity and disability. Recognizing this reality will open the possibility
for us to think through some *realistic* – not *idealistic* – alternatives. One
realistic programme for revolutionary feminist praxis – to borrow from
Marx (1969, p. 282) writing in another context – is, first, to envision a
project for putting an end to class divisions; second, to end exploitative
economic relations; third, to bring to an end all social relations that are
expressions of relations of production including patriarchy and racism;
and, finally, to revolutionize all ideas that correspond to the social
relations of capitalism.

The driving force of capitalist imperialism and thus its fundamental
contradiction is the anarchy of the private appropriation of wealth on
the basis of socialized production constituted through forms of social
difference; this is the enormous ability of capitalism to intensify the
exploitation of the majority of women and men on the world scale
through the organized socialization of production. Revolutionary

feminist praxis constantly interrogates these contradictions, investigating its own analysis and continuously developing itself. But most importantly, as Jazayeri has argued, 'Under capitalism, women's oppression is not a transitional feature. It is everlasting. This makes women a subject of communist revolution – as subject to *become* – just like the working class, which has to become the subject of revolution. But becoming the subject of revolution is a conscious process on the part of the oppressed' (2015, 309, emphasis in original). Education will either contribute to the complex dynamics of the reproduction of imperialism, as it has often done, or be a powerful force in creating a new world free from exploitation, oppression and destruction.

References

Ahmad, A. (1994) *In theory: Classes, nations, literatures* (London: Verso).

A.J.K. (2006) 'On empire: Revolutionary communism or "communism" without revolution?', *A World to Win*, No. 32, pp. 66–88.

Allman, P. (2010) *Critical education against global capitalism: Karl Marx and revolutionary critical education* (2nd edn) (Rotterdam: Sense).

Coulthard, G. (2014) *Red skin, white masks: Rejecting the colonial politics of recognition* (Minneapolis: University of Minnesota Press).

Curtis, M. (2015) *Secret affairs: Britain's collusion with radical Islam* (London: Profile).

Dreyfus, R. (2005) *Devil's game: How the United States helped unleash fundamentalist Islam* (New York: Metropolitan).

Ebert, T. and Zavarzadeh, M. (2014) 'The digital metaphysics of cognitive capitalism: Abandoning dialectics, the North Atlantic left invents a spontaneous communism within capitalism', *International Critical Thought*, Vol. 4, No. 4, 397–417.

Fanon, F. (1961) *The wretched of the earth* (Paris: F. Maspero).

Federici, S. (2012) *Revolution at point zero* (Oakland: PM Press).

Hanieh, A. (2013) *Lineages of revolt: Issues of contemporary capitalism in the Middle East* (Chicago: Haymarket Books).

Hardt, M. and Negri, A. (2000) *Empire* (Cambridge, MA: Harvard University Press).

— (2004) *Multitude: War and democracy in the age of empire* (New York: Penguin).

Harvey, D. (2003) *The new imperialism* (Oxford: Oxford University Press).

Hedges, Chris (2015) *Wages of rebellion* (New York: Avalon).

Hilferding, R. (1981 [1910]) *Finance capital: A study of the latest phase of capitalist development* (London: Routledge & Kegan Paul).

Hinton, W. (1990) *The great reversal: The privatization of China, 1978–1989* (New York: Monthly Review).

Hobson, J. (1902) *Imperialism: A study* (New York: James Pott).

Jazayeri, M. (2015) 'Revolution', in S. Mojab (ed.), *Marxism and feminism* (London: Zed), pp. 305–30.

Johnson, I. (2010) *A mosque in Munich: Nazis, the CIA, and the rise of the Muslim Brotherhood in the west* (Boston: Houghton Mifflin Harcourt).

Khalidi, R. (2004) *Resurrecting empire: Western footprints and America's perilous path in the Middle East* (Boston: Beacon).

Lenin, V.I. (1962 [1913]) 'Backward Europe and advanced Asia', in *The national-liberation movement in the east* (Moscow: Foreign Languages), pp. 82–3.

— (1967 [1917]) *Imperialism: The highest stage of capitalism*, in *Selected works in three volumes, Volume 1* (Moscow: Progress), pp. 673–777.

Linebaugh, P. and Rediker, M. (2000) *The many-headed hydra: Sailors, slaves, commoners, and the hidden history of the revolutionary Atlantic* (Boston: Beacon).

Luxemburg, R. (1951 [1913]) *The accumulation of capital: A contribution to an economic explanation of imperialism* (London: Routledge & Kegan Paul).

Machin, S. (1999) *The age of inequality: Why the gap between the rich and the poor is widening in the age of knowledge, technology and globalization* (London: Orion).

McNally, D. (2009) *Global slump: The economics and politics of crisis and resistance* (Oakland: PM Press).

Mann, M. (2004) *The dark side of democracy: Explaining ethnic cleansing* (Cambridge: Cambridge University Press).

Marx, K. (1969 [1850]) 'The class struggles in France: 1848 to 1850', in K. Marx and F. Engels, *Selected works in three volumes, Volume 1* (Moscow: Progress), pp. 186–299.

Mojab, S. (2011) 'Adult education in/and imperialism', in S. Carpenter and S. Mojab (eds), *Educating from Marx: Race, gender and learning* (New York: Palgrave Macmillan), pp. 167–90.

Oxford English Dictionary (1891a) 'Colonialism' (Oxford: Oxford University Press).

— (1891b) 'Colonial' (Oxford: Oxford University Press).

— (2014) 'Imperialism' (3rd edn) (Oxford: Oxford University Press)

Saccarelli, E. and Varadarajan, L. (2015) *Imperialism: Past and present* (Oxford: Oxford University Press).

Said, E. (1993) *Culture and imperialism* (London: Chatto & Windus).

— (1994) *Orientalism* (New York: Vintage).

Sanchez-Garzoli, G. (2012) 'Stopping irreparable harm: Acting on Colombia's Afro-Colombian and indigenous communities protection crisis' (Norwegian Peacebuilding Resource Centre, Oslo: NOREF). Available at www.peacebuilding.no/var/ezflow_site/storage/original/application/04fcd8f-818b16e1c31c4306ad74dfb70.pdf.

Sassen, S. (2014) *Expulsion: Brutality and complexity in the global economy* (Cambridge: Belknap Press).

Silver, T. (2011) 'Materiality and memory: A Marxist-Feminist perspective on the "cultural turn" in adult education', in S. Carpenter and S. Mojab (eds), *Educating from Marx: Race, gender, and learning* (New York: Palgrave Macmillan), pp. 191–210.

Smith, A. (2015) *Conquest: Sexual violence and American Indian genocide* (Durham, NC: Duke University Press).

Smith, J.C. (2015) 'Imperialism in the 21st century', *Monthly Review*, Vol. 67, No.3, 82–97.

— (2016) *Imperialism in the twenty-first century: Globalization, super-exploitation, and capitalism's final crisis* (New York: Monthly Review).

Wood, E.M. (2003) *Empire of capital* (Verso: London).

Whitehead, J. (2015) 'Imperialism and primitive accumulation', in S. Mojab (ed.), *Marxism and feminism* (London: Zed), pp. 181–202.

Yaqub, S. (2004) *Containing Arab nationalism: The Eisenhower doctrine and the Middle East* (Chapel Hill: University of North Carolina Press).

7

Learning by Dispossession: Democracy Promotion and Civic Engagement in Iraq and the United States

Practitioners and theorists of education have long drawn on the notion of democracy as a purpose, outcome and practice of the discipline. In the years following the US occupation of Iraq and Afghanistan, several important questions were raised about democracy with considerable implications for pedagogy, practice, consciousness and social change. For instance, Ellen Meiksins Wood (2006) and Jean Bricmont (2006) both ask how it is that freedom, democracy, equality and human dignity can seem a convincing justification for war and imperialism. Slavoj Žižek (2002) makes a related point by asking how is it that discussions of inequality and injustice can take place against a 'prohibition' on critical thinking about liberal democracy. For feminist, anti-racist educators, these questions take aim at the heart of our democratic practice. They call into question not only ideology, but also how it is produced and the rigour of its methods.

This chapter brings together Marxist and feminist investigations of two projects on democracy promotion and civic engagement: first, in Iraq, the US project of democracy promotion through networks of women's NGOs; and second, in the United States, the expansive volunteerism programme of the federal civilian national service known as AmeriCorps. By democracy promotion and civic engagement we mean projects on the part of market, state and civil society for crafting and cultivating particular notions of democracy and active citizenship. We draw on a variety of research methods, which will be elaborated in the case studies. However, the projects are united by our use of the theoretical framework we have developed that expands on the feminist and anti-racist extension of dialectical historical materialism into theorizations of education and learning. In taking up this project, we have two inter-related purposes. Our methodological purpose is to advance our understanding of how Marxist and feminist notions of ideology, consciousness and praxis can be used in research. Utilizing these methods, our second purpose is to highlight the conditions of collusion between education and neoliberal imperialist projects for democracy. We will do this by developing the concept of 'learning by dispossession' in order to highlight how these ideological relations are elaborated within spaces of learning. We will begin by triangulating our discussion of the case studies with two important bodies of literature in the field of adult education as well as our understanding of the concepts of citizen, ideology and praxis.

Marxist feminism guides us to make several assumptions in our theorization of learning. First, we regard learning as a historically specific social phenomenon. By this we mean that our understanding and explanation of learning includes our theorization of capitalist social relations. This notion of learning is driven by Marx's articulations of epistemology and ontology, which understand the individual as a conscious human agent participating in particular social relations of production. Consciousness and knowledge are produced by peoples' sensuous experience of capitalist social relations. Thus, we cannot theorize learning solely as an abstract cognitive phenomenon independently of social processes. We try to theorize learning from a dialectical position, meaning that we explore learning as a social phenomenon composed of mutually determining social relations. Learning is, then, a complex mediation of social experience, struggle and meaning-making. In bringing together two projects from disparate local contexts, we will argue that the connection between what is happening in Iraq and the United States goes beyond popularly understood appearances. We base this argument on the assertion that these contexts are particular, but realized through the universalism of the present stage of capitalist development, which we conceptualize as imperialism (see Chapter 6); this invites an articulation of the current global material reality with immense theoretical and political implications. In recent decades, new terms have been popularized to describe the social and economic conditions of our time, such as 'globalization' and 'neoliberalism'. These are, in our understanding, euphemistic namings created in order to ameliorate the harsh aspects of capitalism, in particular its colonialism and imperialism. In this study, imperialism is not simply a form of expansionism or domination, as practised by states since ancient times. Imperialism is the stage of capitalist development, beginning in the late nineteenth century, characterized by the rise of monopolies, the formation of financial capital, the export of capital, and a constant division and re-division of the world into spheres of influence. This stage of capitalism recognizes no borders and engages in war and other forms of violence in order to allow the movement of capital. Neoliberalism means the absolute rule of the market, reductions in social spending, a vast array of deregulations and privatizations, and the transformation of the idea of public good and community. The 'liberal' component of the term hides the harsh reality of the last three decades – wars, genocides, crimes against humanity, trafficking of women and girls, the rise of a new slavery, violence against women, the resurgence of neofascism and fundamentalism, ecocide, growth of the military-industrial complex, increasing poverty, de-industrialization and starvation. While the terms 'globalization' and 'neoliberalism' conceptualize aspects of imperialism, they conceal its destructive, dispossessive urge; similarly, in much academic writing, the two concepts are used primarily in reductionist ways, focusing on continual transformations in culture and communication technologies.

Marxist feminist critique of citizenship learning

Within the discourse of lifelong learning there are several citizens. The first citizen is the catalyst of history and progress, the everywoman or everyman, the poor, oppressed and marginalized. This citizen is the hegemonic identity of emancipation within liberal democracy. The second citizen is entrepreneurial, disciplined, hardworking and flexible. This citizen is the realization of the capitalist ethic. There is also a third citizen, who is the racialized, migrating body, stretched across borders and caught between the lines of nationality. This citizen remains the subject of the project of naturalization, integration/assimilation, and de- and re-skilling. This is not the typology through which educators typically organize their thinking about citizenship and education. Rather, we organize our conceptualizations along the lines of the terrains of citizenship theory (Bosniak, 2000; Schugurensky, 2006) or political philosophy (Usher, Bryant and Johnston, 1997). These typologies have their uses, but what we want to illuminate is the normative argument behind, or usage of, the category 'citizen' and thus our educational interventions. By recognizing that we have three citizens, we begin to understand the contradictory ways in which education is involved in the project of democracy promotion. Thus, our approach is to read them as interrelated social relations.

In the post-socialist, end-of-history political context, citizenship and democracy have re-emerged as central categories of educational theory and practice. John Holst, in his expansive review of adult education and globalization (2007), has argued that the predominant response on the part of adult educators to the collapse of state socialism and the advent of 'third way' politics has been to turn towards civil society as the only hope for democracy. Referring to these educators as, to borrow Welton's term, 'civil societerians' seems apt, as many adopt his assertion that civil society is the 'privileged domain of non-instrumental learning processes' (1998, p. 369). Further, Welton's adaptations of Habermas have had a tremendous influence over the ways in which adult educators conceive the nature of democracy and the role of the citizen in the mediation between 'the system' and 'the lifeworld' as well as the state and civil society. To this end, adult educators have been active in the theorization of social movements and 'globalization from below', in deliberative democracy, participatory democratic methods, and citizenship learning. Similarly, recent calls for a return to the social purpose tradition of adult education have made parallel arguments for the revitalization of democratic learning (Martin, 2008). Finally, the citizen as agent of democratic trans-formation has remained a central category of critical education theories, especially those that advance the rhetoric of socialism but which revert to social-democratic theorization (Foley, 1999; Newman, 2006; McLaren, 2005). As Holst (2002) has argued, the civil society approach embodied in many self-proclaimed 'radical' iterations of adult education has directed attention away from the state as the institutional apparatus of democracy. Further, although we in the field of adult education have been highly critical of the neoliberal reorganization of public policy and its incursion into learning, we have neglected to theorize the relationship between civil society and the state in the promotion of democracy. The 'citizen' is not only a member of civil society, but is a subject of the state and the market as well, and, more importantly, partially mediates the relationship between the three.

Of equal importance to our acknowledgement that organizations in civil society forward their own agendas concerning citizenship learning is the recognition that the cultivation of a particular notion of 'good citizenship' and 'good democracy' is also a historical project of the state. The state – by which we mean the historically specific social relations of government, including its juridical, military and ideological components – engages in a politics of citizenship through a variety of mechanisms. The legal status of citizenship, including the boundaries of naturalization, is established by the state. The state also sets the framework for how rights and entitlements will be promoted, protected and afforded. In tandem with these *de jure* parameters of citizenship, the state also deploys a normative politics through which it promotes *de facto* discourses on what it means to be a citizen. Cultural projects such as the construction of national identity have real material consequences for those who are deemed outside the boundaries of the nation. Historical campaigns to craft the citizenry – such as the Americanization programme in the United States, the mission and residential schools' programmes across North America, ongoing naturalization work across the Americas and Europe, or the Arabization project of the Ba'ath regime in Iraq – are examples of explicit state action in this arena. It is important to recognize that citizenship, as both a legal formation and a cultural notion, is constantly shifting and changing. The boundaries of membership flux and retract and the meanings of membership and participation shift. This is why citizenship and democracy are historically specific notions bound up with larger productive social relations.

Based on our Marxist feminist reading of citizenship learning, we can see that there is a debate amongst educators about the relation between ideology and citizenship learning. However, this debate is confined to the normative content of curricula and fails to address the category of citizenship itself. Thus, if the content of citizenship education is ideology, we ask how is that ideology *organized* and *reproduced* through learning and education? What is the relationship between the ideological content and its reproduction? How does learning and education become a *social practice* complicit in the cultivation of the social relations of imperialism, domination and submission? As discussed in Chapter 4, to engage with this set of questions requires reclaiming different notions of ideology and praxis, different from those promulgated through critical theory and critical pedagogy. Critical educators have been heavily influenced, first, by the Frankfurt School's understanding of ideology, and second, by their own readings of Antonio Gramsci. Perhaps the most common understanding of ideology was well encapsulated by Stephen Brookfield: 'Ideologies are hard to detect, being embedded in language, social habits, and cultural forms that combine to shape the way we think about the world. They appear as commonsense, as givens, rather than as beliefs that are deliberately skewed to support the interests of a powerful minority' (2001, p. 14). In support, Brookfield, in his important attempt to re-insert Marx into critical theorization in adult education, cites a famous passage from *The German Ideology* in which Marx and Engels argued that the class of society that rules over production also rules the production of ideas. This means that the ideas of a dominant group become the 'ruling ideas' of a culture at large and that they are then embodied in hegemonic cultural notions. In this reading of Marx and Engels, ideology appears as ideas and thought content. These 'ideas' are backed up by both violent, coercive practices and everyday cultural forms.

But there is a different way to read this passage from Marx and Engels. The sociologist Dorothy E. Smith (1990, 2004) argued that 'the German Ideologists' to whom Marx and Engels refer were philosophers who 'represent ideas and concepts as if they were powers in and of themselves, whether external to or appropriated by individuals' (2004, p. 448). Ideology, in Smith's reading of Marx and Engels, appears first as the *method of reasoning* of their contemporaries, not as the normative content of their thought. In fact, most of Marx and Engels' adversaries in *The German Ideology* were fellow socialists. It is not the latter's values or purposes that are disputed; it is the methods they use to arrive at their analysis of capitalism and their arguments for political strategy that arise from that analysis. Ideology is picked apart as a method of reasoning that 'means interpreting people's actual life processes as expressing ideas or concepts' (Smith, 2004, p. 448). Only after introducing this understanding of ideology do Marx and Engels go on to demonstrate how these epistemologies result in the production of ideas that support the interests of the ruling class *and* how those ideas are then used to interpret everyday experiences of the social world. This connection between ideas and how they are produced, particularly the general method of academic inquiry taking place within a specific social division of labour, is what is generally missing from our understanding of ideology in education. This reification of the concept occludes ideology as an active process, which in turn divorces ideas and power from how they are actually produced and what they represent. Ironically, this is actually a reproduction of the ideological process.

It is important, and helpful, to remember that Marx and Engels referred to ideology, in this methodological sense, as *negative* (Allman, 2001). This is so not only in the sense that its content is oppressive, but also that ideology performs a negative function in knowledge production. In this sense, ideology *negates* from our thinking the material and social relations that mutually determine our experience and our consciousness; it erases the active human practice that organizes social life and how we think about our life. It erases praxis, the ongoing moment in which how we live, work, think and act mutually determine one another. The revolutionary nature of Marx's philosophy of praxis is in how it demonstrates that ontology and epistemology are dialectically related to one another and historically specific (Allman, 1999). Allman has also argued that, for Gramsci, the notion of ideology referred in part to the search for the origin of ideas, and it is this complex notion of ideology that we bring to the study of democracy promotion on the part of the state and in civil society. We seek to understand not just the normative content of democracy claims, but how educators engage in a method of teaching and learning that performs the ideological functions of negation and abstraction. The two case studies below explore these issues through an analysis of citizenship learning projects in Iraq and the United States. They are distilled from extensive fieldwork on two very complex educational projects. Several years of empirical research have gone into understanding these phenomena. Although a decade has passed since the fieldwork in Iraq, we argue that our analysis is still persuasive despite the considerable change in the political scene of Iraq specifically and throughout the Middle East and North African region more generally.

It is clear that the structural and ideological apparatus for the occupation of Iraq failed; the occupier failed to achieve its objective of 'securing' the conditions for the imperialist appropriation of the natural and human resources of the country. This particular form of imperialist occupation has managed nonetheless to export the destruction of life and society in Iraq beyond its borders to neighbouring countries, and has created the conditions in which the forces of patriarchy, militarism and fundamentalism are strengthened and are ruling throughout the region (see Chapter 6). Under these circumstances, we are witnessing the intensification of all forms of violence against women (Bannerji, 2016), a rise in internal and inter-regional population displacement, and an escalation in internationally migrating populations. In what follows, we discuss selected components of our research projects in the context of Iraq and the United States for the purpose of examining ideological social relations within the institutional imperatives and pedagogical practices embodied in these spaces of learning.

Democracy promotion in Iraq

The imperial wars in Iraq and Afghanistan provided an opportunity to study the relations between ideology and learning in a concrete context of militarized imperialism. The 2003 American project of regime change in Iraq was violent and destructive and has led to more violence and destruction across the region. The war has continued to this day, and it is in fact a condition of continuous war. The United States began the process of solidifying the occupation by launching a number of projects, ranging from (re-)training security and armed forces to the democracy training of women activists. Fieldwork began in 2005 with visits to women's NGOs in Iraqi Kurdistan in order to understand and analyse these organizations' *internal* political, financial and cultural dynamics and to make sense of their activism under conditions of occupation, militarization and war. While visiting the women's NGOs, documentation on their funded projects as well as the curriculum of diverse training programmes for women were collected. One of the documents, *Foundations of Democracy: Teacher's guide* (Rodriguez et al., 1997), was intended as a reference for democracy and civic education training in northern Iraq. This curriculum was produced by the US-based Center for Civic Education (CCE) and was funded by a grant from the Office of Juvenile Justice and Delinquency Prevention (OJJDP) as well as by a grant from the Danforth Foundation. The OJJDP works from the premise that 'Juveniles in crisis – from serious, violent, and chronic offenders to victims of abuse and neglect – pose a challenge to the nation', and that they have to be policed and controlled (US Department of Justice, 2010). This pathologizing logic of the individual as the source of social problems has been critiqued in the work of Colley (2002), Ecclestone (2004) and Pupuvac (2001). This logic serves to reproduce social inequalities by separating the individual from the objective social reality of inequality.

The *Foundations of Democracy* curriculum, in both its 1997 and 2000 editions, was organized around the four principles of authority, privacy, responsibility and justice. It instructed teachers to promote compromise and consensus. The Bible, the Koran and the Torah are presented as examples of sources for moral authority (Rodriguez et al. 1997; Rodriguez and Richard, 2000). The gendered, orientalist and colonialist ideological underpinnings of the *Foundations of Democracy* training manual for teachers (Rodriguez et al., 1997) are best demonstrated in one of the lessons it provides – the story of 'Bill Russell and Red Cloud'. In this story, Bill Russell and Amy Clark, two 'pioneers', are sent to 'negotiate' with Red Cloud and Morning Sun, two indigenous persons from the Cheyenne tribe. Following the story, there is a set of questions about what each of the four characters based their authority on. It is important to note that the only person who derived authority from consent is Bill Russell, representing the white-male-rational thinker – which is to say, the settler or occupier is presented as the authority – who the other pioneers 'consented' to send to the negotiations. His female counterpart derived her authority directly from Russell, who chose her as an assistant. Red Cloud derived his authority from 'custom', and Morning Sun derived hers from moral codes, because 'she possessed great wisdom' and was the spiritual leader of the tribe. This portrayal of legitimate female authority is consistent with the patriarchal, feudal, religious nationalism in which women are perceived as being pillars of moral strength in the family and nation. The story normalizes the genocide of the indigenous peoples of North America carried out by European settlers by describing it as 'conflicts created by the westward migration' (Rodriguez et al., 1997, p. 37); it portrays the 'conflict' as one between two groups having an equal say and power to negotiate, as opposed to the disparate power relations that characterize colonialism and occupation. As such, in the story consent is associated with the colonizer and custom with the indigenous man. In this context, the occupier is represented as the mediator of conflict and the occupied as the guardian of old conflicts. In the 2000 edition for primary schools, the Red Cloud example has been replaced with a narrative about 'Bubble Land'. Bubble Land is a fictional location with non-human characters. In this fantasyland, nonetheless, it is important to learn that 'authority' is necessary or else chaos ensues. This claim is an explicit rejection of the historical development of democracy in favour of an idealist notion:

the idea here is that democracy is not about what actually happens, but rather about principles that float above the 'conventionality' of history.

To discuss, albeit briefly, the ideological content of the curriculum, the analysis here focuses on the relationship between authority and democracy. The 2000 edition of the curriculum states: 'we use authority (1) to protect our safety and our property; (2) to help manage conflict peacefully and fairly; (3) to distribute the benefits and burdens of society; and (4) to maintain order' (Rodriguez and Richards, 2000, p. 39). 'Authority' in this context is constituted as the arbitrator of formal equality, a characteristic of the capitalist notion of democracy. 'In this form of democracy', Allman explains, 'citizens alienate their political power and capacities by handing them over to elected representatives, over whom they have little or no day-to-day influence or control' (Allman, 2007, p. 36). In order to establish this bourgeois model of democracy in Iraq, the occupation was soon followed by the establishment of an electoral system; this is the model of bourgeois liberal democracy that Allman contrasts with the model of revolutionary democracy found in the Paris Commune of 1871, in which 'citizens "reabsorb" their political powers rather than alienating them in the state or political representatives' (2007, p. 36). Iraqi women were expected to use the curriculum in training their constituents for the cause of 'democracy'; they were expected to be both the subject and object of the imperialist restructuring of a country devastated by tribal, feudal, religious and nationalist conflicts. Kurdish women experience these relations of domination and re-domination all at once in an ideologically assembled way. The first National Development Strategy produced by the Iraqi government in 2005 envisioned an agenda that clearly falls within the neoliberal imperialist project; its goal was to 'transform Iraq into a peaceful, unified federal democracy and a prosperous, market oriented regional economic powerhouse that is fully integrated into the global economy' (Iraq Strategic Review Board, 2005).

The US project of regime change was conducted primarily through a high-tech military assault on the country. However, it also undertook a cultural and ideological occupation through the training of women and the funding of their activism by way of a variety of NGOs (Mojab, 2009), replicating the historical trend of co-opting social movements through funding mechanisms (see, for example, Allen, 1970; Incite! 2007; Hammami, 1995). The 2003 war disrupted the existing Ba'ath-dominated educational system but did not replace it with a truly democratic alternative serving the interests of the Iraqi people. As resistance to the occupation grew, Washington launched a project involving the training of pro-American Iraqi citizens who would act to normalize the conditions of occupation and re-structure Iraq into an American satellite state. For example, the American University of Iraq–Sulaimani (AUI–S) opened in 2007 in the city of Sulaimani in the Kurdish region of Iraq. The institution described itself as 'a private, non-profit university offering a comprehensive American-style liberal arts education' with the mission 'to promote the development and prosperity of Iraq through the careful study of modern commerce, economics, business, and public administration and to lead the transformation of Iraq into a liberal and democratic society, through an understanding of the ideal of freedom and democracy' (AUI–S, 2010). Another example is the booklet 'The Role of Organization in Civil Society', prepared by the Ministry for Sports and Youth of the Kurdistan Regional Government (2006), in which civil society and the state are defined from a liberal democratic perspective. According to the booklet, 'civil society' is a sphere separate from the state, the market and the affairs of individuals within the family; it is a sphere where people organize themselves and work together to achieve a common goal. The state is defined as 'a social contract in which people and government engage in a sort of agreement. According to this contract, the state ensures life and security and in return people give up some of their powers' (2006, p. 16). In these two examples, we see the relationships between the state and civil society enacted through particular institutional arrangements; these arrangements bear striking similarities to the case of civic engagement in the United States.

Civic engagement and community service in the United States

Over the last 30 years, a lively academic and popular debate has emerged in North America and Europe concerning the nature of citizenship and, by extension, democracy. Much of this debate has centred on the nature and scope of the so-called 'democratic deficit'. In response to this appearance of a lack of democratic participation in the United States, academics, policy makers and activists within civil society have argued that a new kind of citizen agency is necessary. While various iterations of the 'good citizen' have come and gone throughout US history, today another has arisen in the guise of civic engagement. At the same time that American citizens have been trying to revitalize their democracy at home, the US government has engaged in domestic and foreign policy prescriptions that have advanced the cause of neoliberalism in the United States and spawned imperialist wars in the Middle East. It is in this context that the efforts of the American government to promote 'good citizenship' deserve serious interrogation.

Although seemingly arising overnight following the election of President Obama, this movement for citizen engagement had been building up momentum since the mid 1980s. The civic engagement movement is a broad effort with major stakeholders in civil society, higher education and the corporate sector. The unifying form of this movement is the call for 'community service'. The US government also actively participates in the movement through its efforts to 'activate a culture of citizenship through service' via the civilian national service programmes operated by the Corporation for National and Community Service (CNCS) (Goldsmith and Eisner, 2006), an independent federal agency founded under Bill Clinton, following Al Gore's plan to reinvent government and citizen participation through the proliferation of civil society as a third way for democracy.

Fieldwork to investigate the CNCS began in January 2008 and focused on AmeriCorps, the largest civilian national service programme. AmeriCorps is often referred to as a domestic Peace Corps, and their programmes do bear important similarities. AmeriCorps accepts adults between the ages of 17 and 65 to perform one year of community service at a non-profit organization in exchange for a living stipend and an education award. The education award and the incentive of tuition-loan deferral largely attracts young adults either recently leaving or soon entering university. In this way, it is a substantial act on the part of the government to mobilize American youth. In late April of 2009, President Obama signed into law the Edward Kennedy Serve America Act, which reauthorizes the AmeriCorps programme with plans to expand partic-ipation from its current level of 75,000 members per year to 225,000 members per year over the next decade. In June 2009, the US Congress approved the full appropriation request for the CNCS at $1.14 billion for 2010. This surge of public support for AmeriCorps can be located in the increasing need for volunteer labour following two decades of neoliberal reform and the fiscal crisis of 2009. The community service performed by AmeriCorps members is largely directed at communities that struggle with the devastating effects of poverty, and particularly where public services are unable to meet public need; AmeriCorps programmes target both individuals and the community.

One of the explicit purposes of the AmeriCorps programme is to stimulate citizen participation through experiences of community service. In this regard, civic engagement is considered a measurable outcome of the programme and is assessed at the national level through studies that measure the continued civic engagement of participants after they leave the programme. While each state organizes their AmeriCorps programmes differently, the state where the fieldwork for this chapter was conducted has further named civic engagement as a performance measure of the state's AmeriCorps grant. This means that every AmeriCorps programme operating in this state must produce a civic engagement curriculum, measure its outcomes, and report on these outcomes as part of their funding accountability reports to the federal government. The civic engagement curriculum varies slightly from programme site to programme site; however, each programme must include the following components: 1) a civic engagement 'action plan' in which each AmeriCorps member sets five civic engagement goals to be completed during their term of service; and 2) a set of civic engagement trainings.

The AmeriCorps programme directors who participated in this research engaged their members in a variety of different civic engagement training sessions. The nature of these sessions was shaped by the activities the regulatory mechanisms of the federal AmeriCorps programme allow. The programme is regulated in a variety of ways, including legislation, the code of federal regulations, and congressional rule making. The regulations prohibit a wide variety of activities on the part of the programme director or AmeriCorps member, including engaging in protests, petitions, boycotts or strikes, involvement with union organizing, and, the most nebulous regulation, 'participating in, or endorsing, events or activities that are likely to include advocacy for or against political parties, political platforms, political candidates, proposed legislation, or elected officials' (Code of Federal Regulations, 2005, p. 83).

On the whole, the AmeriCorps programme directors, administrators and volunteers who participated in this research interpreted the above regulation to mean that anything that was 'partisan' was 'political' and that 'political' equated with 'controversial'. During data collection for this project, it became apparent that the programme directors were largely ambivalent about the majority of the regulations. They accepted as common sense the notion that the government is a neutral entity that cannot, in good faith, fund activities with partisan or political values. The regulation that was of most significance to programme directors was the prohibition on participating in potentially 'political' activities, which was interpreted very conservatively. On several occasions the prohibition on 'political' discussions was offered as a rationale for why training sessions were conducted in such a way as to exclude opportunities for volunteers to voice a 'political' or 'personal' perspective. For example, in two separate instances, AmeriCorps members made trips to the state capitol as part of their civic engagement training. In each instance, the members were instructed by their programme directors not to discuss 'issues' with elected representatives. When the groups were asked by elected officials what issues were important to them, the members responded that they could not discuss their perspectives on social problems while 'on the AmeriCorps clock'. They were restricted to discussing why each member of the state legislature had decided to run for office. On the whole, programme directors attempted to avoid critical and personal reflection in training sessions and actively discouraged the sharing of 'opinions'. The sessions were largely confined to acquiring the technical skills needed to complete their community service and to discussions of civic engagement as a vocational activity. However, pedagogical methods for experiential or community-based learning, such as service learning, were not adhered to, thus providing no opportunities for members to reflect on civic engagement activities.

The AmeriCorps programme performs a complicated ideological task. On the one hand, it appears as if there is no explicit framework for civic engagement implemented in the programme, meaning that the CNCS does not hand down such a framework to local programme sites. Programme sites use a variety of curricular documents, some produced by the CNCS and some by foundations, to shape the nature of their civic engagement training sessions; thus, they draw from a variety of institutionalized discourses concerning civic engagement. On the other hand, AmeriCorps members reported that they felt as though there was an explicit and non-negotiable definition of civic engagement functioning in the programmes. This definition, however, was understood by the members to be completely vocational, meaning that civic engagement was something that you 'do' because your community needs it. The parameters of civic engagement were confined to community service and a certain amount of lobbying or engagement with elected officials.

What is significant in exploring the ideological practice of citizenship education, however, is that the notion of civic engagement promoted in the programme was completely divorced from the discussion of controversial, political or partisan issues – meaning that AmeriCorps members discuss democracy as a local, community-based service practice with no exploration of conflict, dissent, coercion, power or interest. This particular understanding of democracy is coupled with an approach to social problems as 'community needs', which can be addressed through rational-technical approaches to augmenting human behaviour and can be accomplished through volunteer labour. This analysis of citizenship and the state as neutral entities is largely influenced by the interpretation of federal regulations by AmeriCorps programme directors under the fear that violation of these regulations will destabilize the programme's public image as a neutral social programme. Thus, the programme functions in a highly politicized environment in which the central dispute focuses on the roots of social inequality. The regulations of the programme confine the relations of learning in the programme in an ideological manner; they rely on the implementation of an abstract conceptual framework of civic engagement and citizenship and discourage reflection on actual experiences of social inequality and difference in their relation to democracy. The regulations, which appear to provide a patina of neutrality, in reality confine the discursive and practical organization of the programme within the hegemonic boundaries of liberal capitalist social relations.

Learning by dispossession

The two cases discussed above lead us to question how democracy promotion and civic engagement projects end up disconnecting and dislocating both educators and learners from their material reality of war, militarization, occupation, social inequality and poverty. This material reality could be characterized by experiences of privilege or marginalization, but is necessarily a gendered and 'differenced' experience based on the specific social location of the individual and their community. In attempting to theorize an explanation for this phenomenon, we have turned to the work of critical educators who have focused on the link between critical pedagogy and the struggle against capitalism and imperialism. This body of theorization does not provide us with the tools to interrogate the ideology of democracy or explain how education, or more specifically democracy promotion and civic engagement, act as active components in the (re)production of the imperialist order. Paula Allman (1999, 2001), Glenn Rikowski (1997, 2007), Wayne Au (2006) and others like Mike Cole (2008) put at the core of their analysis the fundamental contradiction of capitalism – that is, the relationship of labour and capital – and the significance of consciousness in resolving this contradiction. Indispensable as this body of theory is, it does not distinguish between capitalism and imperialism (see Chapter 6) and, more significantly, it does not provide us with analytical tools adequate for the understanding of patriarchy, racism, militarism and colonialism. To address this problem of dislocation from material reality, we have formulated the concept of 'learning by dispossession', a concept drawing from Harvey's (2003) conception of 'accumulation by dispossession' and coupled with a Marxist feminist notion of social and material life.

'Learning by dispossession' is a learning process by which something other than 'learning' – in turn understood as a cognition that can be measured, evaluated or assessed – is happening. So far we have established that learning is a historically specific process of the development of consciousness and knowledge production. We have argued that learning itself is a dialectical social phenomenon. The notion that learning has a dual character is not new to educational theory. In the liberal and pragmatic traditions of education, learning is often established as a relationship between skills and knowledge, reflection and action, theory and implementation. In the critical tradition, this dual character is understood as praxis. This relation, however, is often reduced to a sequential process of reflect–act–theorize. Instead, we argue that the complexity of learning as a dialectical phenomenon means that it has several relations contained within it. One component of this phenomenon is the process through which ideological thinking is organized and reproduced. Harvey argues that capitalism's ability to reproduce itself is contingent on its power to form a relationship between its own reproduction and violent processes of material and intellectual dispossession. From the perspective of education, the continued normalization of capitalist social relations is contingent on the ideological process that 'dispossesses' learners of their own experience.

Thus, much like primitive capital accumulation, learning can produce knowledge and consciousness as well as something 'outside of itself' that deeply entrenches self/mind/consciousness in the perpetual mode of capitalist social relations. To put it differently, 'learning by dispossession' refers to the ways that learning in capitalist social relations produces both new skills and knowledge as well as alienation and fragmentation of self/community. Ultimately, this 'learning by dispossession' confuses learning, or the production of new knowledge, with the subjectification of capitalist and imperialist relations. In this way, the subject of learning becomes the object of dispossession. The liberal ideology of democracy creates the appearance that a progressive, emancipatory educational project is at work, when in reality something else is happening. In this process, the effect of the pedagogical practices of dispossession is to create the conditions through which the learners' experience is presented 'upside down'. Social relations are inverted and capitalist social relations are legitimized, perpetuated, made desirable, and naturalized as *the* option of human social organization. Allman articulates this process as 'ideological thinking' and explains:

> For Marx, ideological thinking/consciousness, at least the type that he calls ideology, is historically specific to capitalism; it is produced by people's sensuous experience of capitalist reality, within uncritical/ reproductive praxis. Ideology serves to mask or misrepresent the real contradictions that make capitalism possible, and, therefore, by helping to perpetuate capitalism, it serves the interest of the dominant class (capitalist/bourgeois) ... The only thing natural about ideological consciousness is that it conforms to the actual separations and inversions of capitalism's real contradictions because consciousness and experience are an internally related unity, praxis. (2007, p. 39)

For example, in Iraq the function of 'democracy promotion' programmes is to position liberal democracy and the market economy as the only possible forms of social organization. In the United States, 'civic engagement' exonerates the state from its role in the reproduction of social inequality and displaces the responsibility for addressing this inequality onto civil society and private citizens. These are two appearances of one phenomenon. On the surface they appear similar in their mobilization of civil society through the utilization of institutionalized apparatuses such as public-private partnerships or particular programme planning techniques. However, their connection is not only in implementation, but in their particularized embodiment of the ideology of liberal democracy. The effects of these practices naturalize local social conditions and obscure alternative social relations. The state remains the neutral arbiter of the market and civil society rather than an active participant in the organization of political consciousness. In both cases, the state organizes the parameters and practices of civil society in such a way that the individual citizen becomes the agent responsible for the success or failure of the democratic project, of democracy learning, as well as of their own material well-being. In this way, the individual citizen is both the agent and object of democracy. The process becomes circular; the purpose of democracy is not the transformation of social life but the production of good citizens. Good citizens are then the guardians of their liberal rights, which are their rights to both equality and inequality. Learning by dispossession is one process through which the ideological practice of citizenship learning transforms the real inequalities and contradictions of social life in civil society into neutral, 'free-floating objects of culture' (Smith, 1990), which exist beyond the realm of the state and which actively organize capitalist social relations.

David Harvey argues that accumulation by dispossession is largely identified by its effects. In conclusion then, in the two cases we have discussed above, our argument is that learning by dispossession functions in a similar manner; the programmes and practices are different, but their common effect is to abstract educators and learners from real contradictions and conditions and to impose the ideology of democracy through the application of conceptual, normative frameworks. From a Marxist feminist perspective, these contradictions are not just instantiations of the abstract labour–capital contradiction, but are processes happening between people who are raced, gendered, classed and sexualized. In other words, these contradictions are patriarchal, gendered, racialized formations of democracy, which disproportionately dispossess those already most compromised in the contradiction between labour and capital, specifically women and colonized peoples. This research is significant for adult educators working for 'social justice' in that it challenges us to question our own assumptions about the horizons of emancipation found in our reliance on the politics of liberal democracy. If we understand that democracy promotion is more about subjugation than liberation and that civic agency is more about submission than engagement, this does not mean that no alternative is available. Revolutionary praxis, explained and made accessible for educators by Paula Allman (2001, 2007), offers us a theoretical base for the undoing of ideological practices in education. The opposite of dispossession is reparation, meaning that what has been dispossessed can, in part, be repaired or returned, and what has been learned can be unlearned, that is, revolutionized.

References

Allen, R.L. (1970) *Black awakening in capitalist America: An analytic history* (New York: Anchor).

Allman, P. (1999) *Revolutionary social transformation: Democratic hopes, political possibilities and critical education* (Westport, CT: Bergin & Garvey).

— (2001) *Critical education against global capitalism: Karl Marx and revolutionary critical education* (Westport, CT: Bergin & Garvey).

— (2007) *On Marx: An introduction to the revolutionary intellect of Karl Marx* (Rotterdam: Sense).

American University of Iraq–Sulaimani (2010) 'About AUI–S: Vision and mission, American University of Iraq–Sulaimani'. Available at www.auis.org.

Au, W. (2006) 'Against economic determinism: Revisiting the roots of neo-Marxism in critical educational theory', *Journal for Critical Education Policy Studies*, Vol. 4, No. 2. Available at http://www.jceps.com/archives/551.

Bannerji, H. (2016) 'Politics and ideology', *Socialist Studies*, Vol. 11, No. 1, 3–22.

Bosniak, L. (2000) 'Citizenship denationalized', *Indiana Journal of Global Legal Studies*, Vol. 7, No. 2, 447–509.

Bricmont, J. (2006) *Humanitarian imperialism: Using human rights to sell war* (New York: Monthly Review).

Brookfield, S. (2001) 'Repositioning ideology critique in a critical theory of adult learning', *Adult Education Quarterly*, Vol. 52, No. 1, 7–22.

Code of Federal Regulations (2005) 'The Corporation for National and Community Service', 45 CFR, Chapter XXV, Subtitle B – Regulations Relating to the Public Welfare (Washington, DC: United States Congress).

Cole, M. (2008) *Marxism and educational theory: Origins and issues* (London: Routledge).

Colley, H. (2002) 'A rough guide to the history of mentoring from a Marxist feminist perspective', *Journal of Education for Teaching*, Vol. 28, No. 3, 257–73.

Ecclestone, K. (2004) 'Learning or therapy? The demoralisation of education', *British Journal of Educational Studies*, Vol. 52, No. 2, 112–37.

Foley, G. (1999) *Learning in social action: A contribution to understanding informal education* (London: Zed).

Goldsmith, S. and Eisner, D. (2006) *Corporation for National and Community Service strategic plan: 2006–2010*, Washington, DC: Corporation for National and Community Service. Available at www.nationalservice.org/strategic plan.

Hammami, R. (1995) 'NGOs: The professionalization of politics', *Race and Class*, Vol. 37, No.2, 51–63.

Harvey, D. (2003) *The new imperialism* (Oxford: Oxford University Press).

Holst, J.D. (2002) *Social movements, civil society, and radical adult education* (Westport, CT: Bergin & Garvey).

— (2007) 'The politics and economics of globalization and social change in radical adult education: A critical review of recent literature', *Journal for Critical Education Policy Studies*, Vol. 5, No. 1. Available at www.jceps.com/index.php?pageID=article&articleID=91.

Incite! (ed.) (2007) *The revolution will not be funded: Beyond the non-profit industrial complex* (Boston: South End Press).

Iraq Strategic Review Board (2005) 'Iraq's national development strategy, 2005–2007', Ministry of Planning and Development Cooperation, Republic of Iraq. Available at www.mop-iraq.org/mopdc/resources/pdf/Planning%20&%20Dev/NDSfv.pdf.

McLaren, P. (2005) *Capitalists and conquerors: A critical pedagogy against empire* (New York: Rowman & Littlefield).

Martin, I. (2008). 'Whither adult education in the learning paradigm? Some personal reflections'. Plenary address to the 38th Annual SCUTREA Conference, 2–4 July 2008, University of Edinburgh. Available at www.scutrea.ac.uk.

Ministry for Sports and Youth (2006) 'The role of organization in civil society', Hewlêr, Kurdistan Regional Government.

Mojab, S. (2009) 'Imperialism, "post-war reconstruction" and Kurdish women's NGOs', in N. Al-Ali and N. Pratt (eds), *Women and war in the Middle East: Transnational perspectives* (London: Zed), pp. 99–128.

Newman, M. (2006) *Teaching defiance: Stories and strategies for activist educators* (San Francisco: Jossey-Bass).

Pupuvac, V. (2001) 'Therapeutic governance: Psycho-social intervention and trauma risk management', *Disaster*, Vol. 25, No. 4, 358–72.

Rikowski, G. (1997) 'Scorched earth: Prelude to rebuilding Marxist educational theory', *British Journal of Sociology of Education*, Vol. 18, No. 4, 551–74.

— (2007) 'Marxist educational theory unplugged'. Paper presented at the 4th Historical Materialism Annual Conference, School of Oriental and African Studies, University of London: University of London.

Rodriguez, K. and Richard, T.M. (2000) *Learning about foundations of democracy: Teacher's guide for primary grades* (Calabasas, CA: Center for Civic Education).

Rodriguez, K., Richard, T.M., Letwin, A.Z. and Quigley, C.N. (1997) *Foundations of democracy: Teacher's guide* (Calabasas, CA: Center for Civic Education).

Sassen, S. (2014) *Expulsions: Brutality and complexity in the global economy* (Cambridge, MA: Harvard University Press).

Schugurensky, D. (2006) 'Adult citizenship education: An overview of the field', in T.J. Fenwick, T. Nesbit and B. Spencer (eds), *Contexts of adult education: Canadian perspectives* (Toronto: Thompson Educational), pp. 68–80.

Smith, D. (1990) *The conceptual practices of power: A feminist sociology of knowledge* (Boston: Northeastern University Press).

— (2004) 'Ideology, science and social relations: A reinterpretation of Marx's epistemology', *European Journal of Social Theory*, Vol. 7, No. 4, 445–62.

US Department of Justice (2010) 'About OJJDP', Office of Juvenile Justice and Delinquency Prevention. Available at www.ojjdp.ncjrs.gov/about/about.html.

Usher, B., Bryant, I. and Johnston, R. (1997) *Adult education and the postmodern challenge* (London: Routledge).

Welton, M.R. (1998) 'Educating for a deliberative democracy', in S. Scott, B. Spender and A. Thomas (eds), *Learning for life: Canadian readings in adult education* (Toronto: Thompson Educational), pp. 365–72.

Wood, E.M. (2006) 'Democracy as ideology of empire', in C. Mooers (ed.), *The new imperialists: Ideologies of empire* (Oxford: Oneword), pp. 9–23.

Žižek, S. (2002) 'Afterword: Lenin's choice', in S. Žižek (ed.), *Revolution at the gates: Selected writings of Lenin from 1917* (London: Verso), pp. 167–336.

Index